Praise for *kinda l*

"*Kinda Like Grace* is a powerful story of amazing transformation. It's what happens when the gospel gets real. With humility and heart, Ginger Sprouse shares her journey from self-interest to self-sacrifice and ends up expanding her idea of 'family' as a result."

Susannah Lewis, humorist and blogger of *Whoa! Susannah* and author of *Can't Make This Stuff Up!*

"What a joy to share a few words about my Gigi and the life-changing read ahead of you!

Be forewarned. *Kinda Like Grace* will capture your heart and challenge your status quo. You *will* cry. You *will* laugh. Your heart *will* be unhinged by the beautiful, unfiltered acknowledgment of brokenness, and you will be cheering at God's redemptive work! I urge you to fully embrace the experience. This is more than a book. It's a call to action, not necessarily to adopt a man from a street corner, but to follow hard after Jesus and allow him to lead you in the purpose he has specifically designed for *you*—to listen for that still, small voice, so that you may answer the call."

Cherrie McBurney, founder and CEO of Covered Media, author of *Covered: A Story of Transforming Grace* and the *Companion Study Guide*, award-winning speaker and Bible study teacher, and certified Elite Mindset life coach

"Profound catastrophic loss of family! That is what is standing on all our street corners. Not by choice but by resignation. The only answer to this mess is a community through the Ginger's, Dean's, and Victor's of our cities. The last thing I needed on my overflowing platter was another book to read. But I could not put this book down. Read it, then go out and jump into that beautiful pungent Bouquet of Christ that assaults our senses yet draws us so close to Him."

Alan Graham, founder and CEO of Mobile Loaves & Fishes, author of *Welcome Home~~less~~: One Man's Journey of Discovering the Meaning of Home*, and host of the *Gospel Con Carne* podcast

kinda like grace

kinda like grace

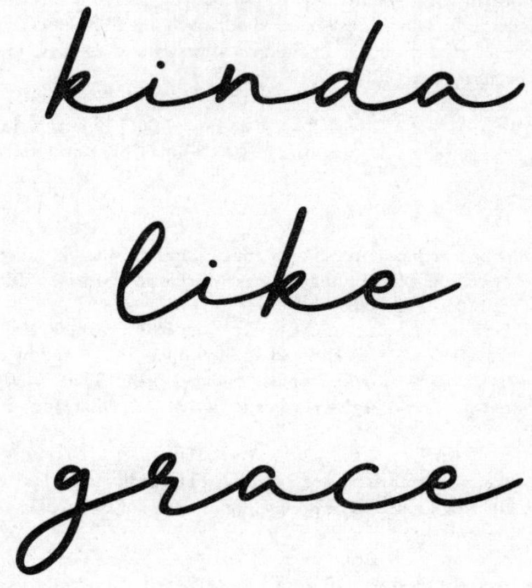

A HOMELESS MAN, A BROKEN WOMAN, AND THE DECISION THAT MADE THEM FAMILY

GINGER SPROUSE

NELSON BOOKS
An Imprint of Thomas Nelson

Published in Nashville, Tennessee, by Nelson Books, an imprint of Thomas Nelson. Nelson Books and Thomas Nelson are registered trademarks of HarperCollins Christian Publishing, Inc.

All photos by author.

Thomas Nelson titles may be purchased in bulk for educational, business, fund-raising, or sales promotional use. For information, please e-mail SpecialMarkets@ThomasNelson.com.

ISBN 978-1-4002-1607-9 (ITPE)

Library of Congress Cataloging-in-Publication Data

Names: Sprouse, Ginger, 1970- author.
Title: Kinda like grace : a homeless man, a broken woman, and the decision that made them family / Ginger Sprouse.
Description: Nashville, Tennessee : Nelson Books, an imprint of Thomas Nelson, [2019]
Identifiers: LCCN 2018048535 | ISBN 9781400207886 (hc) | ISBN 9781400207893 (ebook)
Subjects: LCSH: Church work with the homeless--Texas--Clear Lake City. | Hubbard, Victor. | Sprouse, Ginger, 1970-
Classification: LCC BV4456 .S67 2019 | DDC 277.64/141083092 [B] --dc23 LC record available at https://lccn.loc.gov/2018048535

Printed in the United States of America

19 20 21 22 23 LSC 10 9 8 7 6 5 4 3 2 1

This book is dedicated to my beloved husband, Dean. Without your constant support and patience, I would truly be lost. I'm so grateful to have you in my life, and I am humbled by a God who redeems heart-wrenching brokenness for our good and His glory.

Contents

Prologue

Victor is a sweetheart. In all the time I have known him, I have never heard him utter an unkind word. A big kid in a grown man's body, he is kind, warm, and funny. He refuses to believe anything but the good about everyone he meets. He has an exceptional innocence about him that, frankly, scares me at times. Despite the fact that he is a grown man, he needs help. A lot of help. Depending on the day, he calls me his secretary, his driver, his agent, or his mom. After living on the streets of Clear Lake, Texas, he knows he needs help navigating life.

He has been a fixture in my town for many years. Anyone who drove by the shopping center at the intersection of Nasa Road 1 and El Camino Real saw him. They would talk about "the guy on the corner" with a perplexed tone and wonder about him. Street people in our town were the exception more than the rule, so Victor was an odd sight in our upscale suburban neighborhood, just two blocks from Space Center Houston.

Depending on the day, he would engage in any number of behaviors, from dancing and singing to standing stock-still and staring at the sky. He would also traverse the corner in a tight circle, tapping the light pole rhythmically, and then walk away, only to rush back to tap it again and again and again. He was obviously homeless, but he never seemed to ask for anything. He never held a sign or bothered anyone in the passing cars. He just minded his own business, in this spot he claimed as his own, and spent his days dancing to his own tune, rain or shine. Some said he lived nearby; others said they saw him in different parts of town over the course of many months. I had seen him regularly for three years, although I heard he had been living in the area for eight or more.

I could not tell you what made that particular day different from any other. It was nothing special. Had I known then what I know now, about the road I was to traverse with this man, I cannot say with certainty that I would have stopped.

As strange as it feels to me, many people the world over know me as that lady who met a homeless man at a busy intersection in Texas and invited him to live with her family. It makes me cringe when people say to me, "you're an angel," even when said in utter sincerity and admiration. No, I'm not an angel. I don't want anyone to pat me on the back and give me all the reasons why I should accept the moniker proudly. I want to be honest and tell them that I was a pretty messed-up person at one time.

When my two children were young, the quest for perfection landed me on the bottom of a nasty, lonely, dark pit. And I had no one to blame for the ugly wreck I had made of my life except myself. In the months following my separation from my then husband, Ben, instead of being in my warm bed in our cozy farmhouse, with my little ones tucked in safely upstairs, I was alone, living in a sterile apartment in the middle of the city, sleeping on a hard bed with scratchy sheets, with my head throbbing along with my heart.

It was 2009, and I was about to turn forty. I hesitate to say I was having a midlife crisis because that sounds like an excuse, and many of us have used it as an excuse to sin. I know I did back then. But I don't do excuses. Not anymore. Today I sit here and acknowledge that I'm a person who has always had an aversion to learning from someone else's mistakes, always preferring to make my own.

Funny how with age comes a new way of looking at life.

CHAPTER 1

Victor

It's 2017, and I'm hiding out in my garage "office" in suburban Houston. I don't mean a pretty garage-turned-office from the TV show *Fixer Upper*. I'm referring to a garage office where my desk is my second husband's dusty worktable, and the light is a bare bulb hanging from a cord in the ceiling somewhere above my head. An old Folgers coffee can has found a new purpose as my pencil holder, and my view is of my black Jeep and a colorful multitude of dried-up spray paint cans lining the shelves like soldiers. My giant hulk of a dog, Max, sits under my feet, regarding me solemnly as he idly gnaws on his favorite tattered blue Frisbee. He, too, is lost in thought, likely wondering how much longer he has to wait until playtime, while I'm thinking about the last few years and how it came to be that I'm here, hiding out in my dusty garage with a meditative dog for a companion.

I'm reflecting on all the bad decisions piled up high like the boxes and baskets on the shelves surrounding me. I can say that I possess no self-hatred or condemnation. I'm neither angry nor bitter. I don't need to go to therapy to work on self-esteem issues. I have come to accept who I am: a sinner, saved by nothing else other than the grace of God, and forgiven; imperfect and flawed but loved. I still have a lot of metaphorical boxes and bags I need to sift through, from before my friend Victor turned my life upside down, but all in all, I like this person. I know things could have turned out much, much worse.

My reflection is interrupted by the sudden slam of the back-porch door. I sigh. I've been found. I shake my head ruefully, knowing the locked door serves no purpose other than to pretend I can spend some uninterrupted time alone in my own world. Privacy these days is a rare commodity I treasure. I set my coffee cup gently down on the desk and listen: footsteps crunching through the leaves that have blown across the porch, a shuffle of feet, a light tapping on the door frame, then a firm knob rattle.

"You in there?" a deep bass voice calls loudly through the wooden door.

I laugh to myself and think, *Where else in the world would I be? I don't have anywhere else to hide*. "I don't know, who is it?" I call back.

"It's *Victor*," he says, with slight consternation in his voice. I could almost see his forehead wrinkle.

"Victor? I don't know any Victor. Are you someone selling Girl Scout cookies?" I ask. Then I say loudly, "I don't want any. I don't have any money. Go away and leave me alone. I don't even like cookies." This is our private joke.

Silence, then a loud laugh and more knob rattling. "You so crazy, you love cookies! What you doing in there with the door locked?"

Max jumps up and runs to the door, whining to be let outside. I slide off my wobbly barstool, walk the short distance, and turn the knob. Victor jumps out of the way as Max runs out looking for his ball. I lean against the door jamb, blocking his path.

"What brings you to my office this evening, Mr. Hubbard?" I needle him. I consider it my duty as his self-appointed big sister, even though in reality I'm not so big next to his hulking six-foot-three frame. But there he is, in all his glory, this sweet, dark-skinned child in a man's body.

"I just want to get some snacks out of the refrigerator," he says.

"I'm sorry, Mr. Hubbard, we don't have any snacks here at Sprouse Enterprises, and we're just swamped here in our corporate office."

"What you mean 'office'? This is a garage. You so goofy sometimes." He shakes his head at my seeming confusion and proceeds to brush past me to the rusty fridge for his favorite V-8 juice. The fridge has become his official domain. It's where he keeps all his treats, his special convenience foods that I cannot in good conscience buy for him without shaking my head at the sugar and calorie count. The professional chef in me cringes at the microwave taquitos and the fish sticks served with white bread and ranch dressing. So we compromise, and Victor "shops" in his fridge happily several times a day.

"What you up to out here anyway? Why you out here all alone?" His voice is muffled, as he is headfirst in the fridge. Victor is the most social person I know; it ruffles his feathers when I need a little space in my crowded days.

"Well, little brother, just trying to get some work done," I retort. "But between you and the Girl Scouts, I can't get anything accomplished this evening." My mild sarcasm flies past him unnoticed as usual.

"You need any help?" he asks sincerely, as his head comes

out of the fridge, hands full of juice, fruit, and fish sticks. He is clutching them to his chest like a twelve-year-old boy, and my heart softens as it always does, no matter how irritated I get with him.

"No homie, no help. Just give me about an hour and I'll be inside." I walk with him to the back door and open it wide for him to enter the living room.

"Just an hour, right?" he questions. "Then we can do Bible study time?"

"Yes, sir. I'll be there at eight thirty."

"Okay, don't be late. You know you go to bed at nine fifteen," he reminds me.

"Yes, I know. I go to bed promptly at nine fifteen. You know I'm early to bed and early to rise. I'll make sure I'm on time." This is our conversation. We have it every day without fail. He finds comfort in routine, and I can respect that.

As Victor enters the living room, I poke my head inside and lock eyes with my husband, Dean, who is sitting on the couch with the remote in his hand and our other dog, scruffy little Henry, by his side. He shrugs his shoulders and says sagely, "I told him not to go outside."

I watch Victor lumber across the living room to the kitchen, a solitary peach rolling across the floor behind him.

"I have no doubt, babe." I smile and step across the threshold to give Dean a quick kiss. "Entertain him for a bit, would you?"

He smiles back knowingly and laughs. "It's not *my* attention he wants."

"I know, I know, it's just an hour," I retort as I begin closing the door. I call out across the room to Victor, "Okay, homie, I'm headed back outside. See you in a little while."

"Alright, alright, see you then, yeah," he responds.

He is completely adsorbed with his fish stick sandwich assembly for the moment. I'm relieved, because experience tells me that it will take him at least forty-five minutes to assemble, eat, and clean up afterward.

CHAPTER 2

Noticing

It was mid-May 2016. As usual I was in my car distracted by the traffic, the radio, and applying my lipstick. I wasn't really paying attention. But to my right, as I pulled up to the traffic light, I saw him out of the corner of my eye, dancing near the curb.

I had a rare day off from work and was on my way home after having breakfast with a friend. For once I was in no particular hurry. It was a bright and beautiful early morning, with a cloudless sky and fresh breezes blowing. My car permeated with the smell of my piping-hot Starbucks latte, and I had the sunroof open and the windows down. I was enjoying the wind in my face and one of my favorite songs playing on the radio when I saw him. There he was at the corner of the busy intersection where I had seen him many times before. I was in the lane nearest him, and as I pulled up to the traffic light, I pressed the auto up button for my window. He was no more than five feet from my car, just on the other side of the curb. For some reason, on that particular day my eyes were drawn to him, and I just stared—admittedly,

I would say, quite rudely. I tried to make out if he was talking to himself or singing. He was swinging his arms and seemed to be looking at the cars without really seeing them, if that makes sense. He was not asking for money. He was just, well, there.

He's scary, I remember thinking. If I had been walking, I would have crossed the street to the opposite side. He was tall and rail thin, with ebony skin. His cheekbones jutted out under a matted mop of black hair and a scruffy, matted beard. He had on filthy tan jeans that he was holding up with one hand because they were so baggy, and a stretched-out gray T-shirt with a hole in the front. I remember thinking he probably smelled terrible. As my gaze fell on the ground around his feet, I saw it was littered with bottles, bags, and a lump of something I thought may be a sleeping bag. It had rained the night before and, although the sun was shining brightly now, I was close enough to see the mud squishing between his toes as he did his shoeless marching back and forth. In a rut he had worn into the ground over the months, the puddle splashed as he paced.

I felt my face flush and my heart rate quicken, though I had no idea why. I glanced at the other cars around me waiting for the light to change. Was I the only one seeing this guy? I wondered if he needed anything, being that he was so skinny and without any shoes. My mind kept wondering, *Maybe I should just cruise through the parking lot and get a closer look at him. Okay, I'll stop. No, I won't. Oh, the light is green.* I hit the gas and proceeded through the intersection quickly.

The ridiculous self-talk running through my brain seemed as crazy as the guy on the corner looked. As I drove, my heart rate settled down, and I took a sip of my latte. What in the world was that all about? I had driven by homeless people my whole life, and this guy in particular for several years. While I would feel a certain sadness for them, I never had any desire to stop and check on any of them.

By the time I had reached my driveway, I had determined that the prudent thing to do would be to at least call the police and see if they were aware of this guy and find out what they could do. Being the woman of action that I was back then, I sat down at my desk and had them on the phone in ten minutes flat.

"Webster Police," a brisk voice on the line answered.

"Good morning. My name is Ginger Sprouse. Um . . . I'm not really sure how to put this. This may be a weird phone call, and I'm slightly embarrassed on my part. But I'm calling about this guy on the corner at Nasa—"

"Yes, ma'am, that's Victor. What about him?" Impatience filled her voice.

"Oh," I said, completely thrown off track. "You know him."

"Yes, ma'am, I get at minimum ten calls a day about him," she said.

I sat back stunned. "Well, why aren't you helping him?"

"We can't," she said in a resigned tone. "He's not hurting himself or anyone else. He's not panhandling. At most, the police pick him up periodically to get him off the street for a while, but he always goes right back to that same spot. The mental health aides come by and check on him, but he's an adult. There is nothing we can do."

For the life of me I couldn't accept this. "Isn't there a shelter or family or an organization or something?"

"No, ma'am, I'm afraid not. The family cannot be located, and there are no shelters in the area that deal with single men, only women or families."

"Well, thank you for your time. I don't really know what to do with all that," I told her.

"Neither does anyone else, ma'am," she said, then hung up.

I stared at the phone in my hand, perplexed. Now what?

I continued with my day, cleaning the house, making business calls, and planning cooking events for clients at the cooking school I owned and operated as head chef. As I swept the floor, I thought of the muddy grass Victor was walking through all day. As I made the bed, I thought about the filthy wet sleeping bag Victor would wrap himself in when it got dark. As I folded a load of springtime-scented laundry, I thought of Victor's dirty shirt and his sagging pants.

In the midst of my deep thoughts, my son, Aaron, came home from school. He was a senior, soon to graduate and head off to college, likely a different one than the one my daughter was attending. I watched as he raided the fridge, as was his habit after a long day of books and clubs. I relished the sight of him. Not seeing him every day is a tender, sore place in my heart as he splits his time between his father's house and mine. Each time he comes to spend the night, it seems as if he has grown an inch or two. I looked at his sparkling eyes and the healthy glow of his skin. I listened as he regaled me with the high points of his day and watched as he piled meat and cheese on freshly baked bread and wolfed it down with iced tea and a healthy side of crunchy potato chips. I asked the usual mom questions I always did and laughed at his typical "teenage" responses. He wrapped up snack time, threw away his plate, and wiped a few crumbs onto the floor for the dogs.

"I just swept the floor you know, my boy," I said as I did every day.

"I know, Mom, but look at the pups, they are starving!" He laughed at this and gave me a quick bear hug. "Love you."

"I know, love you too." I squeezed him closer for a moment and counted my blessings.

Calling for the dogs to follow, he left the room, whistling a cheerful tune and jumping high to touch the ceiling as he proceeded noisily down the hall. I sat enjoying the moment, then rose to get a dish towel to wipe the stray crumbs and picked up his glass to wash. As I stood and watched the warm, soapy water drain away, the thought of Victor crossed my mind. Had anyone ever been at home for him? Had he ever had a life with the warmth and love that my family and I shared in this house?

Then I thought back to the phone call with the police department. Was there really no one who could help this man?

CHAPTER 3

Some Soul Searching

Later that night, the dishes were washed, the were dogs fed, Dean was absorbed in a movie on TV, and I was finally in my jammies. Propped up with many pillows in my soft, warm bed, with hot tea on the nightstand, I looked down at the night's reading material in my hand: *The Holy Bible*, with a burgundy leather cover and gold lettering on the binding. I opened it up to the spot marked by the silky black ribbon and ran my fingers over the small print, turning the tissue paper–thin pages idly. My eyes drew here and there to the words, phrases, and verses underlined in various colors over the years, and to my cramped handwriting in the margins.

This very book sat unused on my bookshelf in another house, another life, with another man. I used to pick it up on Sunday mornings after dusting it off as I rushed out the door to go to church, with kids in tow and husband waiting until the last minute to get in the car, tardily putting on his shoes. I would be angry on the way there because we were running late. I would be annoyed during the opening music because someone was sitting in my seat. And I would be irritated because an old friend had snubbed me on the way in for not returning a borrowed item on time. I would open this Bible to the appropriate page during the sermon and maybe underline a passage or two that pertained to someone I knew or something that I was sure to pull out and point to if my husband or children needed some correction. But then it would be snapped shut at the end of the hour and placed back on the shelf at home as I hurried to make lunch and start a load of laundry, so I could have some quiet time for myself, maybe to read a novel or work on the flower beds outside. It would be there, collecting dust, until I needed it again the next week; forgotten, but waiting there nonetheless.

These memories haunt me. Some evenings quiet tears roll down my face over this past life—dead, long gone, and never to return. As they are teenagers now, my sweet babies' childhoods are behind them, as are my hopes and dreams of a picture-perfect family, which I tossed carelessly to the wayside with my choices.

My tea grew cold as I regarded this Bible. For many years it was used as a prop for the life of faith I professed to have. Now it has become my most precious possession. The words contained there had changed me. I turned the pages idly and my eyes fell on James 2:14–17:

> What good is it, my brothers and sisters, if someone claims to have faith but has no deeds? Can such faith save them? Suppose a brother or sister is without clothes and daily food. If one of you says to them, "Go in peace; keep warm and well fed," but does nothing about their physical needs, what good

> is it? In the same way, faith by itself, if it is not accompanied by action, is dead.

As I read, the Spirit of God spoke softly through His Word, right to my heart as He always does, leaving me with a choice to make. I felt the weight of it. I sensed that there was more to do after seeing Victor that day than just making a phone call on his behalf. I sensed that this was an opportunity to look back on the errors of my past, to look beyond myself and help someone who did not have the ability to make choices the way that I had.

My belief in the power of God to redeem lives and circumstances had changed my life and made me a new person. The Lord, through His Word, was convicting me that now was the time to show I was a changed woman, to walk out this faith that I professed to have changed me. Was I willing to be obedient to the call of Christ? I knew there was a possibility that my acceptance would interfere with my life, my comfort, my time, and my relationships. But it was a very clear call, and I knew a decision had to be made.

The call is referred to as "counting the cost of following Christ." Jesus was very clear in Luke 14:25–30:

> Anyone who comes to me but refuses to let go of father, mother, spouse, children, brothers, sisters—yes, even one's own self!—can't be my disciple. Anyone who won't shoulder his own cross and follow behind me can't be my disciple.
>
> Is there anyone here who, planning to build a new house, doesn't first sit down and figure the cost so you'll know if you can complete it? If you only get the foundation laid and then run out of money, you're going to look pretty foolish. Everyone passing by will poke fun at you: "He started something he couldn't finish." (THE MESSAGE)

In the New Testament the disciples clearly saw the cost. They saw Jesus lifted up and crucified. They saw Stephen stoned to death. They saw people who followed the call of Christ cast out of the temple. Perhaps today we have it too easy. Here in the United States, no one is dying for their faith. Most of us, myself included, don't want the inconvenience—at least that was the "Christianity" I ascribed to in my former life.

But this call? It would rock my life and test the reality of this faith I now professed. A long and painful road brought me to this place, and I had a decision to make.

CHAPTER 4

Ginger's Story: Expectations

When I was a young girl, my father gave me the Little House books by Laura Ingalls Wilder. I remember the Christmas morning when I opened the cover of the first book in the series. I was instantly transported into this magical world as the rest of my gifts sat unopened under the tree. I read each book numerous times as a young girl until the pages were worn and falling out. It was a story of a pioneer family that loved, laughed, and endured hard times together, told through the eyes of the author, a young farm girl and adventure-loving tomboy. Our childhoods were similar. I, too, grew up on a farm; the fragrance of my childhood was also scented with freshly baled hay, the sweetest of perfumes; and the sounds of chickens scratching and cows mooing lulled me to sleep at night. The father, a loving yet strong man, was a key figure in the family, as was my own father in my life. And Laura was the apple of his eye, as I was to my father. The books follow the life of Laura from childhood until she marries and has her own little family, seemingly living happily ever after. I wanted to have a life just like hers.

I met Ben in 1996 when I was 24 and he was 26. A tall man with dark hair and arresting hazel eyes, he was kind, sweet, and generous. I was drawn to his calm, easygoing manner and to his family, oddly enough. As an only child I always longed to have a large extended family, with kids running about and joy-filled holiday dinners. Being with Ben and his family seemed like it would give me the life I was sure I wanted. We were married a short six months later.

After our wedding, Ben and I bought a plot of land, built a barn, and had cackling hens running through the gardens and cows in the field. Nicki, then Aaron, arrived in quick succession. I had firm ideas of how I wanted to raise them. I would stay home, homeschool my children, make all family meals from scratch, and become the wife and mother I had dreamed of becoming. It seemed so simple, much like the story of Laura Elizabeth Ingalls Wilder.

I felt so thankful to have the privilege of living out my dream. Simply walking out the back door and taking in a yard full of lush green grass stretching out before me and bright red poppies and magnolia trees bursting with colorful blooms would bring a rush of gratitude. The sound of the door opening would bring a small pack of dogs running around, ready to prance beside me wherever my feet may wander. A look to the left would provide a view of the garden with pole beans stretching up over the top of their poles, looking for a place to climb; head-high tomato bushes weighted down by my favorite heirlooms; and cucumbers curling their tendrils through the fence, almost reaching out, begging to be picked.

There were weeds, too, among the beautiful plants, just like in life. Oddly enough, pulling weeds was always a pleasure of mine; fingers digging deeply into the moist soil to seek out the root and pluck it out. The rows always looked so beautiful when freshly weeded. Tidy, like sweet Nicki when she was dressed up in her Sunday finery, ready to go to church. Many times I would dress her, only to find her outside when it was time to leave, standing in the freshly weeded rows in her white Mary Janes, tomato juice running down her chin, grinning widely as she held one up for me too. I would laugh and have a bite. How could I say no?

I rose early in the morning, grabbed my shining, stainless-steel milk pail, slipped on my favorite pair of rubber boots, then headed out across the dewy yard to the barn, dogs at my heels, fog still lying low across the pasture. I swung the barn door open and saw Mabel, my Jersey milk cow, regard me with her giant, shining brown eyes. She was a sweet one, never asking anything of me, and always a good listener, with wise eyes and a thoughtful demeanor. She was standing at the hay rack, chewing slowly. I stepped up and gave her a pat on the side, then moved my hand up and scratched behind her soft ears. She continued munching, not the least bit concerned about the company in her stall, hay being infinitely more interesting than me.

I reached over the stall door and grabbed a pitchfork to generously refill the hay rack. Mabel moved aside and watched me approvingly, then resumed pulling and chewing. I began to clean the stall, raking and scooping waste into the wheelbarrow. Once fully loaded, I made the trip to the compost pile, carefully balancing my smelly load of manure. The dogs dove into the pile headfirst as usual. I rolled my eyes and laughed. "Why do you think that makes you smell so good? No one is going to want to play with you smelling like that!" I said to them, mentally adding bathing the dogs to my long to-do list for the day. But that was fine with me.

The farm and the work brought me much joy. I loved the outdoors. I still do. The weeding, stall cleaning, grass mowing, cow milking . . . they always made me feel close to God. A gift from my parents, I think. They, too, loved the outdoors and hard work, somehow sensing God's presence in them. I grew up in a church, but the blue sky and the green grass were always the place where I felt the closest to Him.

I was a content wife and mother during those early years. I loved the privilege of having a husband who gladly went to work every day so I could stay home with our children. I had a hot, homemade dinner on the table each night, making sure to sit and eat as a family. I made sure there wasn't too much TV for the kids, and no video games; instead they played outdoors with the pets, got filthy, said their prayers at night, and went to bed exhausted and happy. There was church on Sunday mornings as a family, and Sunday afternoons at Grandma's house. Feeling the accomplishment of providing a loving home for my husband and kids brought me so much satisfaction.

Our lives proceeded this way through much of the kids' childhood. In retrospect, I see that the desire to live my life along the lines of a storybook with a perfect ending created a lot of dissatisfaction within me. I felt it was my duty to make sure we stayed within the script I had written in my mind, which required that I rise early and feed the dogs, cats, horses, and assorted bunnies; gather the eggs; churn the milk into butter; stretch the mozzarella cheese; and grind the wheat for fresh bread. If that weren't enough, I could always find weeds to pull in the garden or vegetables to can for the upcoming winter. And baking cookies was daily on the agenda, as was schoolwork. I homeschooled both of our kids, and that was another full-time job in and of itself. All these things were undertaken with the utmost seriousness by me, not realizing that my desire for a storybook family was wringing much of the fun out of the experience. I had high expectations for myself and everyone around me.

For the most part Ben and I had a quiet, peaceful marriage. We co-parented smoothly; there was no fussing or fighting. He was perfectly content with the way I had arranged our life. In my mind I was an old-fashioned woman who wanted it that way. There were no spa days or shopping sprees for me, by choice. My home was my work, and I was committed to it. I worked hard, thinking it was what I wanted for a long time. So there we were: I, the seemingly satisfied housewife and loving mother, and he, the strong provider of our family.

As time marched on though, there was an emptiness that began to grow in my heart that I could never quite fill through activity; a muted discontent, if you will. After thirteen years of marriage, what looked like a perfect life on the farm was not as fulfilling as I had dreamed it would be. The beauty of the Christian life that I professed to have—the one of love, joy, peace, patience, kindness, goodness, faithfulness, gentleness, and self-control—was woefully lacking. Over time I became bitter, angry, and bored. I looked for faults in others, was short-tempered with my children, and wasn't interested in my husband and his needs and wants. It is painful for me to look back at that woman I let myself become, the one who had everything, yet still wanted more.

To stave off the discontent, I continued in my life of excessive busyness; there was always another project on the farm to distract me. Somehow I thought that it would bring fulfillment, but what happened was I became angry. I was resentful that I had so much to do and so little help. It was not enough anymore that Ben went to work every day and did everything I asked him to do on the weekends. I wanted so badly for my husband to lead, just the way the Bible teaches, and yet I kept a stranglehold on every element of our lives. I had to be in control of everything and everyone, from the rising to the setting of the sun every day. I thought if I did not do everything myself they would not get done, or at least not done "right." I left no space for Ben to lead and undermined his efforts every step of the way, while railing silently to myself about his lack of leadership. My fierce desire to be in control would become my undoing.

I blamed Ben for my weariness, although he never asked me to do anything except love our family. In my heart of hearts, I was angry at myself that despite everything I had, I didn't feel happy. And so I took it out on my family, blaming my husband and even my children. I resented that my kids depended on me, that they loved me better than anyone else, that only my hugs and kisses would do at bedtime. Once upon a time, making cute sandwiches cut into stars and hearts and bandaging random boo-boos had made me feel like the epitome of a good momma. Now I was a hideous caricature of the person I thought I had wanted to be.

I think King David of 2 Samuel 11 would have understood. After many hard years in the wilderness, God had placed him squarely on the throne of Israel. He had all the riches he could ever imagine, many accomplished and beautiful wives, loyal soldiers, and the adoration of his subjects. Even more, he was called a man after God's own heart. Few people have known the sweet fellowship he had with God. His delight in God marked the lines of his songs and the steps of his life. And yet, even he threw them all away—for a fling.

We don't know why David stayed back from battle that spring. One day, as he strolled aimlessly on his palace roof, his unattended heart fell prey to forbidden beauty. But rather than flee from this temptation, he lingered. A look, a longing, an inquiry, adultery, lies, conspiracy, murder, and attempted cover-up. David ultimately repented and found forgiveness from God, but the consequences of his sin sent incalculable ripples throughout the kingdom (Ps. 51).

What happened to David happened to me too. I began to realize that the busyness was not enough, and my thoughts and eyes began to wander looking for something else to make me feel interesting again, noteworthy and appealing. In a novel it might read as an exciting storyline, but in real life, with real people, it's a disaster.

I had decided to have an affair after thirteen years into my marriage. The thought came to me, just out of the blue one day. *Something just for me, no one needs to know, just a secret.* I had been thinking about it for weeks. Thoughts bouncing around in my mind at random times, in between tasks, just waiting for an opportunity to jump into that great abyss, with nothing but inky blackness in front of me. I didn't even know the man yet. I just knew in my heart of hearts it was going to happen. The thought had crossed my mind before; a glance here, a flirtation there. But I always reminded myself that I was a good Christian woman with an image to uphold, and that something like that was for careless, trashy women. I had heard of others falling, and I knew that's what they were. I judged them, turned up my nose in disgust, and thought, *That would never be me*. Never say never, my friend.

CHAPTER 5

Ginger's Story: Dangerous Dreams

It was New Year's Eve in 2008. Mabel, our cow, was in labor, and Ben and I were on standby for the new arrival. As she had been in labor for the better part of the day, I made what seemed like my hundredth trip out to the barn to check on her. It had been raining all week, and the mud sucked at my rain boots as I slogged through the puddles, grumpy and tired. I opened the door and looked at sweet Mabel under the single dangling light bulb. She was snuggled into a thick bed of hay, her belly bulging out to one side. She did not particularly look distressed. In fact, she looked a bit smug. She regarded my irritable face as she continued to chew her cud. We stared at each other for a bit and my irritation evaporated, and I had to smile.

"Everything in its own time, I guess, girl," I said to her. I turned over a five-gallon bucket and took a seat close to her, giving her ears a scratch. Even in the cold, rainy night this barn was my favorite place. Oh, don't get me wrong, it was dusty, thick with cobwebs among the rafters, and smelling strongly of manure, but also of grassy hay and sweet feed coated in molasses.

I sat there with my cold toes tucked snugly under Mabel's fat belly to warm them, leaned forward to prop my chin on my hands, and began to let my mind wander. I thought about how easy it was for Mabel. All she had to do was chew grass all day and wait for someone to feed her. My life, meanwhile, was complicated. I was tired and angry that I had so much responsibility, with Ben, the kids, the animals, the farm, and homeschooling. As I sat there, the roof of the barn that was my refuge seemed to press down on my shoulders. It all felt too close, too familiar, too boring. Surely there was more out there in the world than this little slice of land that I called home.

I thought about all the fun I must be missing on a New Year's Eve: sparkling lights, music, dancing, an exciting kiss at midnight, laughter, and scintillating conversations. I began to feel sorry for myself, sitting on a bucket with no one to keep me company except Mabel, who wasn't much of a conversationalist. The longer I sat there, the more discontent I became. Then I heard the whisper in my ear that night, the same whisper that had started months ago. Had you asked me then, I would have denied it. Sometimes the hardest thing to see is what is right in front of your face. In the silence of the barn, this evening, it was growing louder. I had shrugged it off before, too busy to listen. But here, in this quiet place, it was almost audible.

As I was dreaming of what life would be like outside the farm, the enemy of my soul knew exactly what to say. He told me that I deserved more, that my life was unfair, that God wanted me to be happy. Lies. But much like King David did that day on the rooftop, I sat there and I listened. He is convincing, this enemy. He is eloquent, intelligent, and a diligent observer of our words, emotions, and actions. He spends a lifetime studying us and knows where we are weak, hears our thoughts, and sees our longing gazes at sinful things when we think no one else is looking. He saw my gaze that night, at worldly things, at things outside of my marriage. He spoke boldly and, to my shame, I listened. No, I soaked it in. I welcomed with open arms the voice that told me what I wanted to hear. I relaxed into the arms of the enemy disguised as a friend, and fell for his deceptions, illusions, and lies.

My musing was interrupted by a flashlight beaming directly at my eyes. Ben was looking for me. I waved my arm in annoyance. "Do you mind? You're blinding me."

"I just wanted to make sure you were okay," he said. "You've been gone a long time." There was puzzlement in his voice, along with concern and love.

He had worked all week and had tired lines around his eyes. I saw he was exhausted, but suddenly I was filled with contempt. I embraced it, discarding any shred of compassion or kindness for the man who loved me. I gave myself over to the enemy in the barn that night. He placed a blindfold over my eyes, and I welcomed it like a game, happily, like when I played pin the tail on the donkey as a child.

"I called Steve and Lilly. They're coming over to check on Mabel and see if she needs help. They're bringing Steve's nephew too. They said he's here visiting from out of town," Ben informed me.

I stood and stretched, stiff from sitting on the bucket for so long. I walked to the barn door and gazed out into the inky drizzle. Across the field I saw the beams of flashlights shining over the knee-high grass, and three forms emerged from the woods heading our way.

"Looks like they're here," I said. Then, turning back to look at Mabel, "And looks like this lady here is about ready to get on with it finally."

Steve swept through the doorway first and headed straight to Mabel. Lilly gave a sweet laugh and a quick hug, making introductions. "This is Lucas. He's here to work for us for a while."

Lucas stepped forward from behind Lilly, cowboy hat in one hand and the other outstretched for a friendly shake. "Nice to meet you, ma'am," he said in a soft, slow drawl.

"Nice to meet you too," I returned. "I appreciate you guys coming out on such a cold night, not to mention New Year's Eve," I said with a laugh.

He ducked his head slightly in agreement, and with a "'scuze me" walked to Steve and Mabel to assess the patient.

I turned to Ben. "I guess you should go back to the house and check on the kids. I'll stay here to help," I said dismissively.

He looked at me strangely with his head cocked to the side. "You don't want me to stay and help?"

No, I really did not. I wanted to be alone with my friends, and this handsome stranger who appeared as an answer to my thoughts. "We're good. I'll be in after a while."

He stood for a moment. I could see the hurt in his eyes, but I just looked at him impassively. After a moment he gave Lilly a quick hug and said, "Have fun," then disappeared out the door. Lilly looked at me strangely for a moment but said nothing.

I shrugged and turned to Mabel. "Okay, so what's the status here?"

The next few weeks played out as if in an old black-and-white movie, the reels crackling and splitting. I suspect it's one of those things my mind does not want to relive. It was so shameful that to put it on paper for all to read fills me with horror. But I will, because if even any tiny bit of what transpired in my past speaks to just one person, if it will make that person stop and think, cause them to examine their motives and look beyond themselves, then it is worth it.

During those weeks my everyday farm duties brought Lucas into my life on many occasions. Steve and Lilly were close friends and neighbors, and we always had an open-door policy. Steve had even put a gate in the fence between our two houses some years ago because we visited each other so much. The kids would take cookies to Lilly or go to pet the horses often. We did a lot of life together. And now Lucas was included in our dinners, family gatherings, and game nights.

I would see Lucas as I worked outside in the flowerbeds, watching him surreptitiously as he went about his work fixing fencing and cutting down trees. He would wave politely and go on about his business. I'm ashamed to say, as I sat watching him, many times I would allow myself to daydream about what it would be like to be young and unattached. To not have a pile of dirty dishes waiting in the sink, a mountain of laundry to wash, or assignments to grade. You know. Real life. All the things that need your attention in real life.

When we grow up we have children, homes, families, and responsibilities. But I wondered what it would be like to go back and not have any of those things. To come and go as I pleased, to stay up late, to sleep late, to not have to tell anyone where I was going. The ironic thing was, looking back now, I remember what it was like to be single, lying in my bed at night lonely, dreaming of having a family and hearing the patter of little feet on the floor. I used to look longingly at young mothers and fathers gazing with awe and oozing with happiness over their newborn. It is human nature, I suppose, to never be content with where we are.

I was definitely suffering from grass-is-always-greener syndrome. So, I would rock back on my heels, there among the flowers and green grass, dirt covering my gardening gloves, and brush the hair from my sweaty brow. Squinting into the bright afternoon sun, I would let my mind wander where, as a married mother of two, it had no business wandering. I knew better. I knew, in the same way that when I told my young son not to touch the hot stove because it would burn him, his little fingers would inevitably wander there when I turned my back. Oh yes, I knew. I knew it would burn me, but I did it anyway. But of the devastation, the raging fire that would destroy everything in its path . . . of that I had no idea.

CHAPTER 6

Ginger's Story: Utter Rebellion

I had grown quite attached to my secret longing for this forbidden relationship. I sat in my kitchen with Lacey, a friend from church, and tried to explain myself. I did not speak of Lucas in particular, although I alluded to my thoughts of having an affair. I focused our conversation mostly on my general unhappiness and growing desire to leave Ben. But Lacey was no fool; she saw right through my excuses.

"Just think about my kids," I explained to her. "Why would I want them to grow up in a home with such an unhappy mother? They need to be around love, excitement, and happiness!" I said, dismissing that it was *me* who wanted to be free to find the love of my life and show them the joy of true love.

I remember the way Lacey looked at me, disbelieving, yet with pity and sorrow on her face. She slowly shook her head at the lie I was foisting upon her—and myself. Her silence made me uneasy. I talked a little louder, leaning forward and thumping the table with my hand to make my point, making the coffee cups in front of us rattle. She continued to just sit eerily silent and still, eyes impassive and unreadable.

"Okay wait, I'll get us another cup of coffee. I need to tell you what has been going on these last few months, then you will see!" I jumped from my chair and grabbed the coffeepot from the counter behind me and refilled our cups, my nerves splashing the hot coffee over the edge of her cup. I so desperately wanted her approval, anyone's approval, for what I wanted to do. No, I was looking for permission, really. I wanted someone to tell me that it was okay to leave my husband, against what my nerves and gut knew to be the truth.

Lacey glanced up at me and quietly picked up her napkin to wipe away the spill, and slowly watched as it absorbed the coffee on the table. There was great sorrow in her eyes as they met mine. "I'm not going to give you permission to do this. I am not going to tell you that everything will work out. You're lying to yourself. You have a beautiful family, a loving husband and young children. It will be a disaster the magnitude of which you cannot even fathom," she said, resigned. "I'm speaking to you from bitter experience. Please, do not do this."

I sat back heavily in my seat, for a moment, stunned. This was my friend. Our children had played together for years, and innumerable pots of coffee and cookies had sat in front of us at this very table in my kitchen. We had shopped together, lunched together, and laughed together. This was a person who was supposed to be on my side.

Incredulous, I exclaimed, "Don't you even care whether or not I'm happy? I thought you were my friend!"

"I am your friend. That's why I'm telling you the truth." Her eyes flared, although her words remained quiet and calm. "I hear what you're saying, and I can tell you that using your children as an excuse to leave your husband is the worst kind of lie. It's called deception, and you are drowning in it."

She continued to speak, but I heard none of it. Something dark and angry was boiling up inside of me. I looked at her and saw her lips move but heard only the voice in my mind screaming that she was wrong. The longer I sat there, the more of something that I can only describe as bitter rage took hold of me. "Get out," I said flatly, interrupting her earnest stream of words.

She leaned forward, reaching her hand across the table toward me, beseeching, "Please, just listen to what I'm telling you. The truth is painful, but I'm telling you because I care!"

I looked at her coldly, ignoring her outstretched hand. Then I stood, picked up the coffee cups, and walked to the sink. As I threw the mugs in the sink, the crash pierced the air. I turned to face her, leaning against the counter with arms crossed. I spoke not a word as she sat there helplessly. After a moment, she sighed heavily and rose, unhooking her purse from the back of the chair and slinging it over her shoulder. She slowly pushed the chair under the table and looked back at my glare with calm conviction. "Think about what I said. You can never go back once you do this." Then she turned and walked out.

I heard the screen door squeak as she pushed it open and slammed it shut behind her. Soon after came the sound of her tires on the gravel driveway as she drove away. My self-righteous anger did not allow me to see that I had lost a dear friend that day; it only pushed me closer to what I knew I wanted to do.

I tried once more to get the permission I needed. As my last resort, I decided to speak to my father. As the only child, I was admittedly a daddy's girl. He was really my best friend and had always been there for me. We spoke every day, most days several times. He would stop by on the way to the family farm, somehow always arriving as I was taking out a bread or a sweet treat from the oven. His only requirement was a grandchild on his lap and a cup of coffee on the table. The days of "Ginny," which is what he called me, being the center of attention were long gone; he loved his grandchildren wholeheartedly. His visits were always marked by laughter and messes, kids screaming and running happily, and tickles all around. We had a standing date at Poppi's house on Thursdays, with the understanding that he got the kids all to himself while I made a family dinner.

The kids were up early, always excited for "Poppi" days. They knew that meant running errands, a playdate of some sort, and, if they were really sweet while we accomplished our weighty to-do list, there would be McDonald's french fries as a snack and a hot Starbucks for me, a special treat for all three of us. There was the usual flurry of breakfast, dressing, feeding animals, and packing everything we might possibly want with us during the day. Both Nicki and Aaron loved to read, and so we always had a large bag of books they would spend much of the day absorbed in, which made my life easy. We loaded everything in the car, as well as our border collie, Lucy, and headed out. Ben would meet us at Poppi's after he wrapped up work in the evening.

After a long day of errands, we finally arrived. What had been a bright and sunny afternoon was slowly turning into a gray evening. I pulled up into the long driveway that led to the house and stretched back to the barn and farmyard. I listened to the crunch of the gravel rolling under the tires, a sound I had heard a million times before. The 1930s little white-frame house I grew up in stood proudly before me. The yard was tidy, and the smell of freshly mowed grass hung in the air. Morning glories, with their little faces squashed tightly closed against the evening sky, covered the sagging fence, but I knew from experience that every morning they would greet the world with a riot of bright, violet-blue blossoms.

I had with me the kids, the dog, a bag with all the books, a cup of piping-hot coffee, and a head full of questions and a heart full of rebellion. I was going to talk to my daddy today. I needed to talk about all the thoughts and ideas and feelings I had rolling around inside of me like a roller coaster about to careen off the rails. The dog was barking and anxious to get to the barnyard to chase the chickens; the kids were clamoring to be unbuckled; and I was tired, just weary to the bone physically, mentally, and emotionally.

I sat for a moment and listened to the last few bars of the hairbrush song from Larry the Cucumber, then resolutely turned the key off on the pickup truck. I grabbed my purse and coffee and opened the door, careful to stuff the collie's head back inside until I was ready for his bouncing exit. I circled around and placed the hot coffee on the toolbox in the trunk of the car and opened the door for Nicki. She had tousled hair, a smudge of ketchup on her cheek, and a twinkle in her eye. "Poppi! Poppi! Poppi! Poppi!" she called excitedly.

I turned to see my father strolling down the driveway with his trademark leisurely bow-legged bounce, attired in his uniform of white T-shirt, faded Levi's, and work boots. "Nicki!" he greeted. He had eyes for no one else but his sweet little girl, who was bouncing in the seat waiting for him to come claim her as he had always done since she was just a baby.

"Hey, Aaron!" he said to her little brother with a smile, reaching across the seat for a high five. Then, turning and smacking a kiss on my cheek, "Hi, Ginny."

Nicki, Aaron, and Poppi took off down the driveway, leaving

me with the dog, the books, the groceries, and a mind full of thoughts other than what to make for dinner. I collected my coffee and let the anxious dog out to chase the trio down the driveway. I reached into the truck to grab my purse and, balancing all my items carefully, followed them down the gravel driveway to the house. Tired or not, I was determined to have this conversation.

The night Ben asked for my hand in marriage, I remember Poppi took him into the other room and gave him a "talking to." I asked later what he had said, and Ben told me he said that I was "hard-headed," that I liked to get my own way, and that I was a spoiled only child. Ben told him not to worry, that he could "handle" me. We both laughed. It seemed funny then. But it wasn't funny now.

With everyone fed and Ben working later than usual, Poppi and I sat down for our conversation; coffee was cooling in front of us, and the apple pie was left untouched. From across the kitchen table, I said, "I respect him. I'm just tired. I feel like I'm the only one working hard. On the farm, in marriage, whatever. I respect him. I just don't think I love him anymore."

My daddy rocked back in the kitchen chair, which squeaked angrily. He picked up a pencil from the table and began to draw on the napkin in front of him, not speaking. After a few moments he looked at me. "You don't respect him. If you did you wouldn't be thinking about another man. You've already crossed the line. You're already involved, whether you have done anything or not." It wasn't a question but a strong statement. "You better think long and hard about what you're thinking. You'll ruin your life, and the life of your kids and Ben, not to mention your mother's and mine. I don't want to have to face all of my friends and tell them my daughter ended up divorced because she had an affair." He said it angrily.

I would say we were very close. We spoke every day, but we rarely shared feelings in our family. I was sitting there pouring out my heart, looking for guidance, and my daddy, whom I loved dearly, was concerned that I would embarrass *him*? The enemy of my soul was there again, whispering in my ear, "Time for some pride here, dear one. Doesn't he care about you at all?" I pressed my lips tightly together to hold back my sharp retort, because I was taught never to talk back to my daddy.

He continued to watch me, suddenly standing and walking to the sink. He stood for a moment and straightened as if making a decision. "If you leave Ben, if you get involved with this man, don't bother to come back here. I stand beside Ben and the kids, and you will not be part of this family anymore."

I stared, stunned and speechless.

At that moment Ben breezed through the door, late from work, smiling. "Hey guys, what's going on? Any dinner left?"

I leaped up from my chair. "It's in the microwave. I'm not feeling well. Can you please eat and bring the kids back home with you? I'm leaving. And can you stay and hang out here with *your* dad? I don't know what happened to mine."

"Sure," he said, puzzled. "Can I stop and get you any medicine?" he asked in a concerned voice.

"No, I'm good. See you at the house." Ignoring my father, I grabbed my purse and slammed the door behind me. I drove home that night in a blind, angry rage.

I made my decision that night. In my anger and pride, I gave myself over to the enemy of my soul. I will never forget it. It changed the course of my life from solid rock to sinking sand.

That night, after everyone was in bed, I sat at the kitchen table in the dark. I thought about my dad and his refusal to listen, my own anger, and Lacey's advice. I also thought about Ben, what I wanted out of life, and how alone I felt. The house was quiet, except for the dog snoring on a pillow beside the table. My closed laptop sat in front of me. I looked at it for a long time that night, with my hands in my lap, not touching it. I knew what I was going to do but felt afraid. The longer I sat and thought, the more my heart began to beat in my throat. I could feel it pounding.

As if on their own, my hands reached out and opened the laptop. I typed www.facebook.com, placed the cursor in the search box, and stared at its blinking light. The keys clicked loudly as I typed Lucas's name, then boldly, I clicked "Add Friend."

Almost instantly I saw the response "Friend Request Accepted" and a box pop up: "Hey, how are you, my new friend?"

And so it began. Just like that. A name in a box. A click of a button. Lives shattered. And words said that could never be taken back. Oh, I'm not deceived anymore. It had started months ago in my heart, and it's what made it easy. What is in a person's heart is what comes out. He did not pursue me. I had decided wholeheartedly that this was going to happen. The ugly brazen harlot that the Bible speaks of made an appearance, and I blithely stepped aside and let her lead.

Very late that night, with adrenaline zinging through my veins from my conversation with my new "friend," I went to bed in my favorite PJs, an old army T-shirt of Ben's. It was raggedy, soft, and cozy. I wrapped myself up on my side of the bed with the pillow and blanket tucked "just so" under my cheek. Usually getting them just so required at least five minutes of tossing, fluffing, and adjusting; all of which Ben always tolerated with the utmost patience. It was just another bratty and selfish move on my part. Somehow I thought it was fine to pull the blanket from him, untuck it to make myself comfortable, and adjust it according to my taste.

It was typical in my marriage: I, many times the tyrant; Ben, tolerant and gentle. It's embarrassing and humbling now to look back and hear the tone and tenor of the tune that we danced to in those days. It wasn't the sweet music couples dance through life with but a clashing and banging of cymbals and drums. My tune, a sweet melody it was not; yet he smiled and listened anyway.

One would think that having someone love me right where I was, who allowed me to have my will and way, would instill appreciation and love in me. But, alas, sometimes humans don't function that way. What it did was cause me to get angry, like a child begging for boundaries, ever pushing, pushing, and pushing, hoping the parent will say in a commanding, resounding voice, *No!*

I was immediately sucked into the affair. It was only purely emotional at this point, but I wanted more. I would wake up in the morning, say good-bye to Ben, and hurry to feed the kids and start them on schoolwork so I could check my messages. I was short with everyone, impatient and annoyed that they were wanting and needing me. It quickly turned from clandestine messages to texts many times a day. And then came the fateful day when we met face to face for the first time since our Facebook chat. It is shocking to realize that it took just one encounter, an inappropriate flirtation, to end up on a tumultuous slide down a mountain without brakes or a safety net at the bottom. Just utter destruction. It makes me sick to write about this, and I feel so ashamed.

Even now, there are times when I see my children struggling. Although they are nearly grown, in my heart they are still my babies. There was a time when they desperately needed and wanted my attention, but so often now they don't want my help. I'm still earning back their trust, and rightly so.

King David knew this all too well. He had to face the consequences of his rash decision to possess something he had no right to have. Nathan, the prophet of God, said to him in 2 Samuel 12:7–12:

> The LORD, the God of Israel says: I anointed you king of Israel and saved you from the power of Saul. I gave you your master's house and his wives and the kingdoms of Israel and Judah. And if that had not been enough, I would have given you much, much more. Why, then, have you despised the word of the LORD and done this horrible deed? For you have murdered Uriah the Hittite with the sword of the Ammonites and stolen his wife. From this time on, your family will live by the sword because you have despised me by taking Uriah's wife to be your own.
>
> . . . Because of what you have done, I will cause your own household to rebel against you. I will give your wives to another man before your very eyes, and he will go to bed with them in public view. You did it secretly, but I will make this happen to you openly in the sight of all Israel. (NLT)

When I think, *Oh, that I could have those moments back*, I bet David thought that too. But we cannot go back. If only I had not been so consumed with myself, full of the sickest kind of sin.

I see the damage I had caused and feel helpless that I cannot go back and fix it. I want others to know that the excitement fades, feelings change, and people come and go. But the self-loathing and the loss of relationships that really matter will be damaged beyond repair.

I told myself that I would get divorced, marry this man I so wanted, and take my kids with me. That everything would be fine. Those people who warn you otherwise? The magazine articles and therapists that tell you how damaging divorce is? I believed they were all wrong, because for me it would be different. It mattered not that other families had difficulty blending, because mine would be different. And God would forgive me, because He says He forgives our sins if we ask. I just needed to get past this hard part and then I would go back to Him. Oh, I knew that the Scripture says there are consequences. But I wanted to be happy! And God wants me to be happy, right?

Ben said I had no empathy. He said I didn't possess any of it, not even a shred, when I told him I wanted a divorce. He accused me of having an affair and that I was abandoning him, our two children, and our home.

It was just another weekend day in 2009. But the words spoken that day would provoke a drastic change in me. I can still recall how the sun came up bright and beautiful that morning, just like it does most summer days in Texas. I drank my coffee, fed the kids a short stack of homemade blueberry pancakes, then told Ben that I was leaving him. Just like that. No drama, no gut-wrenching revelations, no expletive-filled fight with Grandma's dishes flung against the walls. After months of inner turmoil and angst, it was as anticlimactic as a lit firecracker that fizzles and flares and then lies limply in the grass.

"I just don't want to be married to you anymore," I said to my weeping husband. I had to speak quietly, because the kids were in the nearby master bedroom, snuggled up in blankets in the "big bed," watching Saturday morning cartoons. Ben and I were standing in the middle of the living room, toys and books scattered around our feet. The cat was curled up on the windowsill, sleeping peacefully in the sunshine, and the dog was scratching at the door, waiting to be let outside.

Ben stood there before me, with his hazel eyes red-rimmed and the pain of my words etching deep lines on his face. I couldn't look at him. I walked to the door and let the dog out, then paused for a moment, leaning my forehead on the cool glass. I gazed outside, wishing I could run away like the dog, bounding across the yard, without a care in the world and, certainly, no one's feelings to consider.

I took a deep breath and walked back to where my husband stood with his arm hanging limply at his sides. Tears were still falling silently and dripping from his chin. I didn't know what to do or say next.

"Want a cup of coffee?" I asked inanely, unsure of where to take the conversation.

He stared at me as though I had lost my mind. "Really? That's what you have to say? Do I want a cup of coffee?" he hissed. "No, I don't want your damn coffee. I want my wife! I want our life back! I want my children's mother to be here, every day when I walk in the door. I want your love, your time, your attention. I want this nightmare to go away!" He said these words in a loud whisper, through clenched teeth, then stared at me as the restrained rage in his voice vibrated through the air.

"Mommy!" My seven-year-old daughter, Nicki, was standing in the doorway. "Can I have some juice?"

Ben's back stiffened as he walked to the kitchen, rubbing his eyes. He stood silently in front of the sink, hands balled into fists on the countertop, staring straight ahead.

"Sure sweetie," I was finally able to get out. "Apple or cranberry?" I asked with false brightness.

As I filled her cup, Nicki ran to her daddy's side and wrapped her arms around his legs, bouncing up and down, dangling there as she often did, laughing up at him. He turned his face down to look at her and ran his hand over her tousled blond locks, cupping her sweet pink cheek in his hand. I watched him take in her sparkling green eyes and her favorite faded Barbie nightgown, now much too short for her.

She then ran to me, grabbed the cup, and hop skipped back to her cartoons, shouting, "I love you, Daddy O! Thanks for the Juice O, Mommy O!"

Ben continued to stand there, still and tall as a redwood tree. Then he straightened further, took a long, ragged breath, and blew it out. He turned and walked slowly to where I stood in front of the refrigerator. I felt afraid. He was a gentle man, but he did not look gentle at that moment. I could only imagine what was going through his mind. Was he going to punch me? Wrap his hands around my throat? Scream obscenities in my face? He stood for a moment looking at me, as though he had never seen me before. It was true. All the ugliness that had grown inside me was right there in the open between us.

His voice shook as he quietly let out, "You have no empathy. You have no heart. You want out? Then get out." He turned on his heels, picked up his keys, and walked out the door. It snapped shut with a terrifyingly final click. I was instantly afraid of what I had done. I slumped back against the cold stainless steel of the refrigerator, feeling both scared and relieved that he was gone. My mind traced back over the last thirteen years of our marriage. It was not entirely true that I did not want to be married anymore. I did. But ever since I had become involved with Lucas, what I really wanted was a do-over. A new start. A fun, laugher-filled life that I thought I would find with someone else.

My ears had become so attuned to the voice of the enemy of my soul that I could hear nothing else over the roar of his voice. Not my children's cries, not my husband's tears, not my father's angry lectures. My heart had turned to stone, and I relished it. I held it up before my eyes and imagined it a sparkling diamond, rare and rich, a treasure to behold. But it was just glass, something that would shatter when dropped, common and ugly like my thoughts.

Ben and I were separated for three long years while I carried on my affair. Me wanting out of the marriage; him unwilling to let go. As I chased my new idea of happiness, I had become a different person—even more self-absorbed, if that were possible. Desperate for attention, I dressed seductively, drank heavily, and spoke harshly.

Many conversations and tears had passed under the bridge. Ben and I sat in therapy together one evening—he forlorn, me stubborn and angry—when the therapist looked at him and said, "If she does not want to be here, then I can't help you. I can't make her love you back." That was the end.

In the parking lot I told him, "I don't want to be married

to you anymore." Then I turned and walked to my car. I think that was the day that his tears stopped falling; instead he became angry and bitter. Who could blame him? The family he had lovingly poured himself into was ripped away from him, and he had no say in the matter.

The manipulation of the kids began, as it does in so many marriages gone awry. The sweet innocents who were bruised and perplexed were used as pawns in a game of control by their parents. It was then and is now a sickening way to treat the children we profess to love. It is as if we use them as some sort of a buffer between two warring parties.

The litigation began soon after. I was terrified of going to court and having all my dirty laundry aired before a room full of strangers. The ordeal reminded me of the very thing that God had promised to King David in 2 Samuel 12:12: "You did it secretly, but I will make this happen to you openly in the sight of all Israel" (NLT). We went to mediation, and somehow during that time we divided the kids: sweet son for him, darling daughter for me. My heart remains broken to this day that I allowed that to happen. What followed was years of pitting them against each other. I only hope and pray that God will heal the hurt that I inflicted on the ones who lost everything; the scars are still visible even today.

One night, while standing on the balcony of my lonely apartment building in the middle of a city I hated, I leaned heavily on the rusty railing, regrets swirling about my head like mosquitoes. With a stiff drink in one hand and a cigarette in the other, I lifted my eyes heavenward as a hard lump formed in my throat.

A certain Scripture passed through my mind, memorized many years ago:

> God has called us to live holy lives, not impure lives. Therefore, anyone who refuses to live by these rules is not disobeying human teaching but is rejecting God, who gives his Holy Spirit to you. (1 Thess. 4:7–8 NLT)

So there it was, hanging out there in the open between God and me. I opened my fingers and watched the cigarette fall, glowing brightly as it hit the musty leaves below. *Maybe it will start a fire*, I thought idly. *And I will burn up, like my beautiful life.* Feeling I did not deserve to live, I thought about ending my life that night. My old friend, the enemy of my soul, was there again, whispering in my ear. He thought it was a grand idea. I was getting tired of his voice. I could dimly remember what the voice of the Lord sounded like, just that it was still and small, kind and loving. This other voice, the enemy's voice, was raspy and loud, crass and crude. There was no love there, just a mocking laughter at the reality that I had believed his lies. My life lying in smoldering ruins proved it. There was a chasm between God and me that night; perhaps it had been there all along.

I stared into the dark. Then I saw a figure beckoning me from across an abyss, with hair as white as snow, just as He is described in Revelation 1. He smiled and nodded encouragingly, holding out His hand, just standing there, not moving. He wanted me to come to Him, to trust Him. All I needed to do was take the next step. It is our trust in putting one foot in front of the other that causes the path to appear beneath our feet.

But the longer we stand and ponder, the longer we shoot our darting glances below, the more our resolve begins to weaken, our earthly thoughts begin to rise up, and our sinful logic sets in. We begin to think of how to escape the path we are on: *If I just carefully hold out my arms and balance, I can put one foot behind the other and slowly back away from this fearful sight in front of me. It's too far to the other side, too hard to get there, but this side is really okay. I know it's supposed to be amazing over there, but really, it's not for me.* The truth was, I was afraid. Oh yeah, I was afraid.

The healing began from there. In my lowest point, I saw the truth.

It was 2011, two years after I had asked for a divorce, and things were still hard. I was working full time and spending as much time as possible with my children. Lucas was long gone, never having had any intention of spending forever with me. It was a rude awakening, but one I desperately needed. My relationship with my father was still strained but getting better. I knew I had hurt Ben beyond any kind of relationship, so we grimly gritted our teeth and communicated for the sake of the kids. The one thing I was so very grateful for was that we stopped bickering and agreed to focus on the children.

That spring, through a friend, I met Dean, who was also reeling from a recent divorce. At the time, neither of us was in any kind of emotional or spiritual place to start a relationship. But slowly, our mutual pain drew us together, and against any kind of common sense (we laugh about it now), we married the following year.

It was in our home, a new place we created together after the Lord had wrought miraculous healing to both our lives, that I felt the call to help Victor as I read my Bible. This home is where I had finally learned, after all that painful time, to look beyond myself and see the pain of others. And most of all, to be available for God's purpose.

CHAPTER 7

Stopping Changes Everything

I'd like to say this is the part in the movie where the *Rocky* music begins to play softly, then rises to a crashing crescendo as I rush in and change Victor's life. However, as often happens in the light of the morning, the rising sun in the window shined light on the heart in a new way.

After a night of restless thoughts, I rose early as was my routine and sat at the kitchen table with my coffee and my Bible. That day the pages almost fell open on their own to Mark 12:31: "Love your neighbor as yourself." I sat with that for a while, searching my mind for an excuse. I thought, *Technically, Victor is not my neighbor.*

I stood from the table, moved deliberately to the sink, and washed my cup while looking out the window at the green grass and the school bus rolling by. I then walked toward the bedroom, picking up shoes and fluffing pillows on the way. I set the Bible on the end table by my bed, picked up my purse, checked my lipstick, and very deliberately scrubbed the thought of Victor from my mind.

I took Aaron to school and, driving the long way around the city center to avoid the corner altogether, found myself in a yoga class at the gym. I stretched and posed, and even "oommed" a little bit. I felt great. I was running a little later than I would have liked, but no problem. After a quick dash home and a shower, I headed out to start my day and get to work.

Preoccupied with thoughts of what I wanted to accomplish, I proceeded on my regular route to the cooking school. Have you ever gotten in the car and arrived at your destination without paying attention to where you were going? One of those "how did I get here" moments? As I was sitting at the traffic light to turn onto the main road, guess who went dancing across my line of sight? Yes, Victor. I slumped quickly down in my seat, hoping he wouldn't see me. I swear, it felt like his eyes were right on my car. I reached up and pulled the visor down, made a quick right, and headed to my cooking school, feeling like a complete failure as a human being. So much for putting the subject out of my mind. *Yes, he is your neighbor*, the still soft voice whispered in my spirit. I was so disgusted with my cowardice that I slammed my hands on the steering wheel and said loudly, "*Fine!* I'll stop!"

I made an illegal U-turn and pulled into the parking lot behind Victor. As I maneuvered my car back toward him, I saw him turn from watching the street to me. I stopped and rolled my window all the way down. Almost as if he had been waiting for me, he began to walk toward my car. I wondered about the wisdom of stopping to talk to a street person, but quickly consoled myself with the thought that we were in broad daylight at one of the busiest intersections in town.

As he headed toward me, he made a sharp turn to the right at the last minute before coming to the car window. I watched him do what I later learned was his routine: turn from the corner, kneel down, touch his left shoulder to the ground, walk in a straight line to the car, turn, walk all the way to the back left side of the car, touch the passenger-side door handle, then traverse back around the front of the car. As he walked to my window, he said in a deep voice, "I'm Victor."

I had thought before that he looked scary, but up close he did not. He was thin and, yes, he smelled bad, but he was smiling shyly. The kind of smile that makes your eyes light up and crinkle at the corners.

"What's your name?" he continued, sticking out his hand for a friendly shake. I hesitated a moment, then placed my manicured hand into his. His hand was very sticky, and I noticed his nails were long and dirty. Up close he smelled worse than I had imagined.

"I'm Ginger. Pleased to meet you!" I said, thinking how surreal the interaction was. I remember feeling relieved that he seemed fine and could carry on a conversation.

"How are you today?" he asked me as though we were old friends who had been apart for just a few days.

"Well, I'm great. Um, how are you?"

"Oh, I'm doin' alright, alright." He continued, "Where you headed today?"

"I'm headed to work. I just wanted to stop and see if you needed anything."

"No, I'm good, I'm good. I don't need anything."

Really? I thought. *Nothing? Cause you're dirty and smelly, and yesterday I saw you walking shoeless in the puddles.*

Almost in response to what he could not have heard me

thinking, he said, "Naw, I don't need anything. I'm just glad you stopped. It's good to have somebody to talk to."

I thought I could give him five bucks and be on my way. But out of all the needs he had, he just wanted company. Interesting. We talked for about ten minutes. I stayed in my car and kept the door closed. But all my reasons for not stopping had dissipated with the warmth of his smile.

"Well, I guess I'd better be going. Glad you're okay. Glad I stopped," I finally said.

"Yeah, yeah, me too! When you coming back?" he asked with a big smile.

"What? Oh, I'm not sure. I was just stopping today. I hadn't thought about it. I guess I can come back tomorrow." *Oh, me and my big mouth.*

"Yeah! That'd be great! What time will you be here?"

At this I was thinking, *How would he know what time when he doesn't even have a watch?* But I pressed on determinedly, "How about lunchtime? Want me to bring you something?"

"Yeah! That would be great! How about McDonald's?"

This is doable. I can grab him lunch, swing by, drop it off, and be on my way. My conscience will be assuaged, he will be fed, and all will be right with the world. Success! Or so I thought. "All right, lunch tomorrow it is. Would you like anything in particular?"

This question prompted the beginning of a lesson in the ways of Victor. He said, "A double meat burger with cheese. No onions. But pickles are good and jalapeños. Large fries with extra ketchup and a shake. But tell them all three flavors. Vanilla, chocolate, and strawberry. It has to be all three."

"Oh, okay, but I'm pretty sure you need to pick one flavor. What's your favorite?"

"No, no, no. It have to be all three. Mixed up. In a big cup."

"Really? Well, okay, I'll see what I can do, but no promises."

He stood there until I started the car and shifted into gear, then he told me to stay safe.

I smiled and nodded, "Of course I will."

"Don't let nobody do you no wrong," he commanded. "See you tomorrow." Then he walked away.

"Yes, yes," I nodded, "looking forward to it."

I slid down in my seat to absorb what had just happened. When I sat up and put my sunglasses back on, I saw Victor standing in the same spot on the corner, evidently intent on seeing that I was safely back on the road.

I ducked my head slightly and gave a wave, feeling relieved to be driving away. I thought about it all the way to work. *I don't have to stop again,* I told myself. *How would he ever know anyway? There must be dozens of Jeep Cherokees that drive by that corner every day.* I even thought up a few new routes I could take to work and to my son's school that didn't include passing by that particular corner.

With Victor's fast-food order firmly fixed in my mind, I was irritated that a street person would be so picky about his lunch order and did not recognize that I had taken time out of my busy day to stop and talk to him. At the same time, I felt incredibly overwhelmed by his need. What good would a burger do for this guy? He needed way more help than I was willing, I'm ashamed to say, or, more importantly, equipped to give him.

While at work I could not get my mind off Victor on "the corner," as I was beginning to refer to his home base in my mind. I pushed my chair back from the desk and kicked my feet up on a pile of recipes waiting for my attention. I stared at the ceiling and reflected on my quiet time of last evening and this morning, and my calling as a Christian. I thought about my faith and what it meant to say I was going to follow Jesus. I thought about my willingness to "count the cost." I thought back again to John 14 where Jesus spoke to those following Him. Would I be willing to give up my home, family, money, or convenience? Would I? I knew that was the question I had to answer. Was I willing to go out of my way to help someone else at such cost? To step out into the smelly, messed-up world of a stranger? Right then and there I prayed, *Lord, I'm not willing, but I know You can give me the willingness to reach out if that is what You are asking of me.*

The butterflies that had been dancing in my stomach suddenly sat still. I felt a warm wash of peace flood my mind and settle my nerves. I nodded, as I was solidly confident of what the Lord wanted me to do. *Why make him wait until tomorrow for that burger?* I heard Him ask. I stood quickly, and before I could change my mind, I grabbed my keys and purse. I slapped off the light switch as if to slap away any remaining doubts in my mind about helping this man in some way or another. By God, if nothing else I was going to start with that hamburger and shake. The certainty of doing the right thing was zinging through my veins as I started the car and drove down the street to McDonald's.

I turned into the back of the long lunchtime drive-through line, feeling peaceful about my decision. After waiting patiently, I pulled forward and stated my somewhat complicated order into the black box by my window.

"You want three milkshakes? Chocolate, vanilla, and strawberry?" the voice queried.

"No, I want all three flavors in one cup, mixed up with a straw," I repeated.

"I'm sorry, ma'am, we can't do that. But I can give you three shakes if you like."

I sighed, then restated my order once again. "Yes, double meat, make sure there are no onions, and yes, three flavors in the shake. I understand they all come out separately, but could you just stir them up please?"

"I'll have to ask the manager on duty if we can do that. One moment please."

"Oh, well, okay. Yes, please ask him," I said to the air. The gentleman behind me who had been patiently waiting until then gave a sharp honk for clogging up the long lunchtime line.

The voice from inside the box spoke again. "Ma'am, if you could pull up to the side so we can get the line moving, we will get an answer on that shake for you shortly."

"What? Oh, okay, I guess so," I said, and sighed. *Wait! Really? I came here to get Victor a burger, but seriously, this was getting embarrassing.* I decided he would have to make do with one flavor. I pushed the button to get the drive-through attendant's attention and called out, "Never mind. If you would just do the best you can, I'll take whatever."

"I'm sorry, ma'am, please pull to the side."

I pulled over out of the way, jammed the car into park, and crossed my arms, frustrated. Not so many minutes ago I had been all in, ready to make Victor's day and do something good, something that would make me feel good too, not to mention doing what the Lord had plainly asked me to do. Now, a little thing like a shake was causing me such irritation that I wanted to scrap the whole idea and drive away.

I flipped the visor down to check my lipstick but stopped and looked at myself. My hair was pulled into a high ponytail with wispy strands framing my face, and my blond highlights sparkled from the sunshine streaming through the sunroof. My dark brown eyes complemented well with a pretty, new liner I had purchased a few days before, and my favorite red lipstick rounded out my everyday look nicely. *No, it's not the shake. It's you. You with "much,"* I thought to myself as I stared in the mirror. "From everyone who has been given much, much will be demanded; and from the one who has been entrusted with much, much more will be asked" (Luke 12:48). All of a sudden, the lady I saw in the mirror was not so attractive anymore. I realized this was not about a burger and fries and shakes. It was about putting someone else before me.

There was a knock at the window. It was the manager with a bag and the shake in his hand. As he passed them through the window, he asked, "Is that shake by any chance for the guy on the corner down the street? The homeless guy?"

I looked up, surprised. "Yes, it is! Do you know him?"

"No, I don't know him," he replied, laughing a bit. "You're just not the first person requesting a tri-colored shake, so I figured it must be for him. Quite a few people have come through the line with the same order in the last few years. I threw in a few apple pies; he likes those too. And ketchup. He likes extra ketchup."

I paid and thanked him, feeling slightly embarrassed and very humbled as I drove away with my tri-flavored shake. Apparently, there were other people looking out for my new friend as well. Somehow that made me feel better.

I pulled into the parking lot behind Victor. He proceeded through his routine of pacing around the car and touching his shoulder to the ground, then he bounced up to the car excitedly. "Where were you? What took so long? I thought maybe you forgot!"

I was just here an hour ago and told him I would be back tomorrow, I thought to myself. I raised my eyes heavenward and cocked an eyebrow at the Lord. I wondered if He was laughing at me. "Well, Victor, just lots of people wanting shakes today. Want some company?"

"Yes! I would love company!" He ushered me to his corner and opened his arms wide. "Have a seat, anywhere you like!"

I looked around at the ground littered with trash, and the muddy grass bent from the weight of his bare feet pacing back and forth for days on end. I will leave the fragrance to your imagination. I took a deep breath and eked out a "Thank you so much," then sat carefully on the grass, in the driest spot I could find. He placed his hot lunch and shake on the ground next to me and began to pace back and forth, scanning the cars diligently. I watched him for a few minutes and asked, "Would you like to come eat your lunch?"

"Naw, I'm alright, I'm alright."

"You're not hungry?"

"Naw, I'm good, I'm good."

With a sigh, I sat there on the grass—on the smelly, dirty ground—in the sunshine, next to the fragrant burger and the melting shake. It seemed he had little interest in his lunch or my company. After sitting there for half an hour just watching him pace, I finally stood and said, "Well, I guess I'll go. It was good to see you."

He stopped his pacing immediately and politely walked me to my car. Holding the door open for me, he asked, "When you coming back?"

The sweetness in his question and the hopeful look on his face broke my heart. "How about Friday?"

"That sounds great! What day is this?" he asked me, smiling happily.

"It's Wednesday today," I answered, as I smiled back at him.

"Okay, great, I'll see you then Friday. What time?"

Wow, I thought, *there is no getting off the hook with this guy*. "How about 10:00 a.m.? I'll bring coffee."

"Oh, no, I don't drink coffee. I like cocoa from McDonald's. With whipped cream and extra cocoa syrup in it, and chocolate sprinkles on top. In a big cup."

I swallowed my laughter and said seriously, "You got it. I'll be sure to remember that."

He shook my hand and carefully closed my door, checking to make sure it was securely latched and that I was tucked safely inside. He stood there waving as I drove away. I squinted into the sun until I couldn't see him anymore. I gripped the steering wheel tightly and took a deep breath. *Okay Lord, I'm in. But I'm not going to lie, I'm going to need You every step of the way.*

That evening I made chocolate chip cookies. It's our house favorite. As my sweet son, Aaron, my loving husband, Dean, and I sat around the table discussing life and how our day went—our after-dinner chatter always makes me feel warm and happy—I dropped my bombshell. "So, Aaron, you know that guy that stands on the corner that we see all the time?"

"Yeah, what about him?" he asked. They both knew right away who I was talking about.

Before I could answer, Dean asked, "What's the deal with that guy? He looks mad, and he's always waving his arms around and talking to himself. He never asks for money, though, it's weird. He's been there for as long as I can remember."

I swallowed. "Yes, that guy. His name is Victor. I stopped and talked to him today. In fact, I took him lunch." There was dead silence as two sets of wide eyes locked on my face in astonishment.

Recovering quickly, Aaron jumped in immediately. "Mom! What's wrong with you? Didn't you always say it's not safe to stop and talk to strangers? What were you thinking?"

Meanwhile, my husband sat back, spinning his iced tea glass between his fingers and regarding me with amusement on his face.

"I call myself a Christian," I explained myself. "And it's my job to take care of my neighbor. I did not have any other choice but to stop and check on him."

With Aaron bouncing on his seat asking a million questions and Dean just quietly observing and eating warm cookies, I told them about my day's adventure with my new friend.

CHAPTER 8

A Friendship Is Born

As the days flowed into weeks, I began stopping by regularly to check on Victor and to see if he needed anything. Although I knew he was there on the corner by choice, the question that really nagged me was why? What was up with that spot? I knew there were panhandlers around town who had spots staked out to hold up their signs and ask for money. But Victor did neither of those things. He had no interest in anyone's cash; he was always happiest for some company. So why there? I was baffled.

One weekday afternoon, after a particularly busy day, I found myself and my ever-present cup of coffee on the corner watching the cars go by with my new friend. It was a rare day when he would sit on the ground beside me instead of pacing restlessly. For whatever reason, that day he had a calm air about him, and we were enjoying some conversation about family and friends. I say conversation, although he had difficulty maintaining what I would call a normal dialogue. Most of the time he would answer only if asked specific questions, and sometimes he would change the subject. But this day, he seemed willing to talk.

"So, Victor. Where are you from? Around here?" I queried.

"Naw, I'm from West Texas."

"West Texas? That's kind of far. How did you end up here?"

He sat there quietly for a moment, watching the cars. "My momma is here. She moved here and I came here to be with her."

I sat for a moment looking at him. Then, perhaps a little louder than I should have, asked, "Your mom is here? In town? What in the world are you doing here on this corner if your mom is here?"

"Well, I . . . I . . . I mean she is here. I just don't know where she is," he stammered.

"When is the last time you saw her?" I asked quietly.

"I don't really know. A month?"

I was confounded. His mother saw him here in this spot, in this sorry state, and did nothing? "Why didn't she take you home with her?" I asked, but without giving him time to answer, I began peppering him with more questions. "Where does she live? Do you know her phone number? Does she work? Where?" I thought maybe I could find his mother and get him some help. But the more questions I asked, the more Victor began to shrink away. I stopped and took a deep breath. "Okay, Victor. What's her name?"

I pulled a phone from my pocket and began to make notes: name, phone number, last place he knew she had lived, and last place of employment. I was also horrified to learn he had a sister in town as well. In fact, she lived so close to where we were sitting, we could have walked there.

When pressed about his sister, he told me that he knew

exactly where she lived. He had walked there once and knocked on the door. "She couldn't let me in. Her landlord told her not to let too many people inside."

"What?" I asked incredulously. "That does not sound right, Victor. Besides, even if that were the case, she could have stepped outside to talk to you."

"Naw, naw, it's alright," he protested. "I don't want her to get in trouble."

I raised an eyebrow and let that one go. I was beginning to see as our conversation progressed that he was very protective of his family, particularly his mother. I realized that if I wanted him to give me any kind of information I was going to have to respect that, regardless of what I thought. As we spoke that day, though, one thing that really began to sink in was the fact that he had difficulties with time and dates. He said he had been on the corner only for a few months, but I knew for a fact that I had been passing him for several years. I knew it would be difficult to keep track of time while being on the street, but it seemed a bit extreme. I told him I would start looking for his mother that afternoon.

"How? How you going to find her? I walked all over the city and knocked on all the doors we used to live, and I went to her work and I can't ever find her," he said sadly.

I was perplexed by the whole idea that she knew where he was and yet was still nowhere to be found. Nevertheless, I promised him that day that I would do everything I could to find his mother.

At that point, although I had been sitting beside him the whole time, he finally turned and looked me in the eyes. "You think you can do that? I been waiting so long."

It finally dawned on me. "Are you on this corner because you're waiting for your mother?" I asked gently.

"Yeah, this was the last place I seen her," he admitted.

He was worried that if he stepped away from the corner, he would miss her when she came back for him. Of all the reasons I had thought as to why he was on this street corner, I hadn't thought of this. Why would anyone rather sleep on the side of a busy intersection, in a sleeping bag saturated in rainwater and sweat, than in a clean bed?

I knew then there was much more to his story. This grown man—thirty-two years old, six feet tall, and thin as a rail—needed his mother. I decided I would do everything in my power to make that happen.

I was confused and angry that his mother had left him. I thought surely there must have been a misunderstanding. In an effort to give her the benefit of the doubt, I thought perhaps she had been hurt and was in the hospital, or maybe she had told him to meet her somewhere else and she was waiting frantically to hear from him. But in my heart, I knew they were unlikely scenarios. Victor needed help. A lot of it. It would be overwhelming for anyone. But the Holy Spirit reminded me that my job was not to judge but to be kind and compassionate.

Fall arrived, and I knew we needed to find some sort of shelter for Victor before winter came. The nights were turning cooler, and his physical condition was deteriorating. Some days he could carry on a semblance of conversation, marked here and there with otherworldly references to clouds, star signs, and God. He assured me God was watching him so I didn't need to worry; he was not alone. Other days I would greet him and he would just stare at me blankly as though he had never seen me before.

I would ask him questions and he would mumble something unintelligible, then walk back to the corner and just stand there stock-still. Those days were especially painful for me.

His uniform for many months had been a dirty white T-shirt and someone's cast-off khaki pants. His shoulder blades jutted painfully sharp against the thin material of his shirt, and his pants would slide slowly down his legs if he forgot to hold them up. I knew from prior calls to the local police department that many people had complained about the man "exposing" himself on the street corner. And I was not the only one who had supplied him with a belt; he had a collection of them on the ground around his area.

His feet, too, were an issue. His tennis shoes had been in such bad shape, with the soles falling off, that he had to eventually abandon them. They lay forgotten among the trash strewn about his corner. There were also several new pairs on the ground with the old ones, given by others. When I asked why he didn't wear those shoes, he responded that they were the wrong color.

"Well, what color would you like? I can get you those."

"Blue," he answered matter-of-factly. "Dark blue, Nikes, basketball shoes."

I was surprised at his quick, clear response. "Do you know what size you wear?"

"Thirteen and a half," he said. And just like that, he turned around and resumed his usual place facing traffic. It was disconcerting when he behaved this way, but I was learning that conversation some days was harder than others, so I made sure to ask pertinent questions first.

"I'll be right back, okay? Don't go anywhere," I joked to the back of his head.

No response. I shrugged and walked to my car. I could find

size thirteen-and-a-half Nikes, even if everything else seemed so hard. After a quick trip to the sporting goods store, I returned less than an hour later. Victor bounced up to the car as if he had not just seen me that day. I rolled down the window and, holding up the bag, asked, "So, Victor. Do you like presents?"

His dirty face lit up. "What you got?"

"Oh, just a little something I thought maybe your toes would appreciate," I said, smiling at him.

He backed up as I opened the door. I walked to the back of the Jeep, lifted the door, and made a place for him. "Here, I made you a spot to sit."

He hesitated.

"Don't worry, you're not going to get anything dirty." I patted the cargo area.

After sitting down, he opened the bag and removed the box of shoes.

"Try those on and let's see if you really are a size thirteen and a half."

I stood in the waning afternoon sun watching him tear into the box like a child on Christmas morning. He pulled out the Nikes and turned them over and over in his hands, examining them carefully.

"They are real Nikes?" he questioned, somewhat suspiciously.

"Yes, sir, straight off the shelf. Here are some socks. Try them out."

I winced a little as I watched him pull the sparkling white socks over his dirt-encrusted toes. I had not thought to bring anything for him to clean up with. I noticed his dexterity was a bit difficult, so I helped him with the socks and the shoes. With his foot on my knee, I laced them up as I had done so many times for my children. I thought how this grown man still possessed the same childlikeness that my kids had grown out of. His grubby fingers with overgrown fingernails were an incongruous sight on the clean laces as he tied an "extra good" double knot.

He stood and turned to me, bouncing on his toes. "Perfect," he proclaimed. "Thank you!"

He surprised me with a big hug. I confess, I held my breath, as he was really quite fragrant. But that aside, the smile on his face was enough for me. I bid him good evening and told him I was headed home. He was still bouncing when I pulled into traffic.

There were many mornings I would bring Victor a hot cocoa and breakfast taco only to stand near his dew-covered sleeping bag in which he was rolled inside like a burrito. He was just a few feet from the curb, the morning traffic rushing by, and the grass wet beneath his new Nike basketball shoes. I wondered how in the world anyone could sleep with the sirens blaring and horns honking, and with his foot hanging off the curb into the street.

Occasionally, the mound of damp fabric would be unbelievably still. Each time that happened my heart would rush to my throat, and I would cautiously call out, "Victor, Victor, hey, you awake?" Then I would nudge him with my toe, hoping he was still breathing, but at the same time thinking, *What if he's dead?*

I would stop and check on him late in the evenings on my way home from work if I didn't see him standing in his usual spot when I passed by in the morning. Every time, even after a long day, I would make the U-turn and go on a search, knowing there would be no rest for me until I was sure he was safe for the night. If not on the corner, many times I would find him in the alley behind the upscale sushi restaurant in the adjacent parking lot. He had a certain kind of peace on his face when asleep, without the worried wrinkles that lined his forehead. With his tired eyes finally still from the constant scanning and looking all day and his long lashes resting over them, a sense of calm prevailed, even as my headlights illuminated him on the ground in the dark of the night.

The apartment where he had last lived with his mother was on the other side of the fence. He would sleep jammed up as close as he could to the broken wooden fence, with his head tucked deeply into his hands, placed just so under his head. I thought many times that he looked as though he were trying to will himself back into his old bed, in his old apartment just a stone's throw away. Perhaps he was dreaming of his old room and belongings only to wake up to the stench of urine, the clanging of pots from the restaurant kitchen, and workers staring at him on their cigarette breaks. I imagine him rolling over in the morning and opening his eyes expecting to be at home, then seeing his surroundings with resignation.

Like clockwork every day he would roll out and be back on the corner in time for the morning rush hour. Pacing, singing, and waving his arms just like the day before. On occasion he would stop at a Subway on the trek across the parking lot to his corner. Bless the employees there who would always treat him with kindness and a free meal when he, smelly and dirty, sidled up to the counter and placed his order, while the other customers in line stepped back several paces from this wild-looking man. Leaving any place with doors always required much tapping and touching on the way out, much to the consternation of anyone walking out behind him.

To watch him eat his sandwich was always a study in balance.

He would lift the quivering tower of fillings toward his mouth, seldom noticing that they had cascaded down over his shirt onto his lap. Hands covered in mayo went unnoticed as well as he lifted his large Mountain Dew to his lips to wash it all down. Leaving the table and bench in a mess, he would duck his head, throw up a peace sign, and walk quickly the other way.

He would then head back across the parking lot and take up residence on "his" corner, spending the rest of the day there looking for his mother.

While Victor maintained his vigil on the corner, I spent my evenings scouring the internet for his mother. I looked for phone numbers, prior addresses, social media, but nothing surfaced online. It was like she was a figment of his imagination. I went to the store where he last remembered she had worked, but no one seemed to know or remember her. The clerk at the police station knew Victor but expressed they, too, had tried and failed to find his mother. As a last resort, I went to the apartment building where he told me they had last lived. The desk clerk knew instantly who I was talking about when I asked at the building office.

"Victor? Yes, I know him well. He and his mom lived here for about eighteen months a few years back," she said. She told me his mom would go to work every day, leaving him home alone. But then he began roaming the property while she was at work, causing some of the residents to complain about his dirty clothes and the way he was always looking around, like he lost something. And so the management kicked him out, leaving him to spend the days roaming the streets around town. Then about two years ago his mom stopped paying her rent and eventually got locked out of the apartment.

"You should have seen that place. Filthy and dirty, rotten food in the refrigerator. She wanted to come back and get her stuff, but management wouldn't let her. I don't know what happened to her. But that's pretty much when Victor moved to the corner full time. I guess he just didn't have anywhere else to go," she told me.

She said many of the shop owners and people in the area have gotten to know him, and they all watch out for him as much as they can. Sometimes he would come back to the building and she would give him candy. "He's sweet, if smelly. But harmless."

I was shocked to hear about his mother. But this gave me hope that she was alive somewhere, and I was determined to find her. Surely there must have been some sort of misunderstanding. How could someone just leave her own flesh and blood?

CHAPTER 9

Happy Birthday and Merry Christmas to Me

It was late 2016, and I continued to search for Victor's mother with little success. He thanked me politely whenever I offered to take him downtown to a shelter, and we agreed to disagree every time he told me, "No, thank you."

Christmas was approaching, as well as my birthday. As I stood on the noisy street corner on this chilly weekday afternoon, I watched Victor from behind my dark sunglasses. I was getting to be quite good at making one-sided conversation. As I rambled on in my usual cheerful fashion, I told him my birthday was coming up, and that I was going to be forty-six this year.

He tore his gaze from the passing cars and looked at me for a change, surprise written all over his demeanor. "Forty-six? Wow! You look so young."

"You think I look young, huh?" I lifted my hand and shoved my sunglasses on top of my head so he could see my eyes. How could I not like this guy? Without even thinking about it, I asked him if he would like to come to my birthday party the next night.

"Well, of course," he said. "I would love that." With those words he gave a firm nod and turned back to the traffic. I felt victorious that I had elicited some emotion from the man.

"All right then, I'll have my husband Dean pick you up tomorrow at 7:00 p.m., since I'll be at Art of the Meal cooking up a big dinner. It'll be in the evening, is that okay?"

"I'll be here."

"All right. Then I'll see you tomorrow evening, Victor."

No response this time, but I had learned not to be concerned. I knew he would be ready and waiting.

The next day, in my commercial kitchen at the cooking school, I wondered about the wisdom of my impromptu invitation as I washed, chopped, and baked the day away. I had no idea how my guests would react, or for that matter how Victor would react. I had only seen him eat at Subway, and not exactly with a mother's table manners.

I had invited my mom, my two teenage children, Dean's parents, and a few close friends for the birthday dinner that night. I didn't tell anyone about my special guest until everyone had arrived. I warned them that Victor may not smell amazing, as he was living on the street, and asked them to just please welcome him as a gift to me.

"The guy that stands on the corner all the time waving his arms? That guy is coming to dinner?" Ron, one of my more outspoken guests, exclaimed. "Is he even safe?" he queried, taking a large gulp of his Merlot.

"Yes, he's safe. He's my new friend. We hang out," I replied with a smile.

He looked at Dean, who was heading out to pick up Victor. "You good with this?"

Dean laughed. "He's harmless. See you in a few."

Victor's arrival at my party that night is burned into my memory. It was fully dark outside. The candles were lit, and the Christmas lights inside the cooking school were twinkling though the plate-glass windows. The table was set with a crisp white tablecloth, the good china, crystal wine glasses, and flowers. The aroma was drool inducing, being that I had been cooking up a feast all day. So, with the dinner and the cake ready, we all waited for our last guest.

Victor arrived in fine style, wearing a pair of heavy overalls that someone had given him and the blue Nike shoes I bought him, and smelling like the bottom of a dumpster in mid-August. The funny thing was, this man had not a care in the world. He walked in smiling and waving as if it were a welcome party in his honor. (Dean related later that he was waiting on his corner like he was awaiting his personal limousine.) He greeted each of the guests in turn with a manly handshake, then taking the person's hand, placing his other notably grimy hand on top of theirs, and stooping down a little to look at them right in the eye, asked each and every person, "What's your name?" After he had greeted everyone in that way, he turned and gave me a huge hug.

"Happy birthday!" he shouted.

"Well, thank you so much. I'm so glad you could join us!" I smiled, holding my breath just a little. I was happy to see him and was astounded by his sweet and gracious manner. I motioned for him to bend down so I could whisper in his ear, "I brought you a change of clothes if you want to put them on."

"Sure, that sounds great," he said.

Smiling, he lumbered down the hall toward the bathroom with the paper sack I gave him. He was obviously with his full faculties that evening. I watched him amble away, then turned back to a room full of big, round eyes. My guests were standing awkwardly, wine glasses in hand, staring at me as if I had suddenly lost my mind.

I smiled brightly. "Appetizers anyone?"

As I passed the platter with fancy amuse-bouche, I felt a certain giddy satisfaction that Victor seemed fine, and I was happy he was there. The discomfort my guests felt was of less concern to me than making sure that Victor had a great evening, and that he felt welcome. I suddenly realized why I had been anxious about the evening. I was so concerned about what everyone else would think of him—his odor, his manner, his missing front tooth—that now that he had arrived and it all seemed fine, I was finally able to relax. He made his second entrance for the evening in his much cleaner attire, and by this time everyone had, for the most part, composed themselves and had resumed chatting.

Dean's sweet mother swept in and took over. "Victor, can I get you a glass of water? How about some appetizers?" she asked with her lilting Southern drawl and kind smile. He towered over her tiny five-foot frame, and with her blond hair and blue eyes, they were an incongruous sight.

His eyes lit up. "That sounds great!" he exclaimed. He bent carefully over the appetizer tray as she patted him reassuringly on the back.

She caught my eye with a wink. "We're all good here, darling," she called to me.

I gave her a huge grin. "I see that. Thank you." *That lady got it all right. The grandkids didn't call her Precious Granny for nothing.*

I turned to my other guests and called everyone to the big round table, where all ten of us would be sitting together as we had many times in the past. As we gathered and joined hands to pray, I glanced around at the small group of friends, at all the faces of those I hold near and dear to my heart. It was a true gift to me that no one had anything negative to say about my guest of honor, at least not to me. As we bowed our heads to pray, I watched Victor out of the corner of my eye, not being sure how he would respond to the group prayer. My heart smiled as I heard his "mmmm hmmmms" of agreement, followed by a hearty "Amen" at the end.

As we passed plates and piled them high that night, I cringed just a little as Victor wolfed down his food, ate with his hands, and dropped parts of huge bites here and there. I saw Precious Granny hand him a napkin and quietly remind him to wipe his mouth. I don't think I had ever been more grateful for my sweet momma-in-law. Under her watchful eye, the dinner was uneventful, if not a bit messy on Victor's part.

My guests sang "Happy Birthday," and we all enjoyed the cake and ice cream. Victor beamed so happily that one would almost think it was his party. After I had refused the many offers to help wash the dishes and clean up, my guests began to drift out for the evening. I lingered over the small mountain of dishes, a task that has always been relaxing to me, while Victor and Precious Granny chatted like two happy magpies over a cup of warm cocoa.

Later Dean wandered in and asked, "Think it's about time I take him back?"

I leaned out the door and looked. Precious was putting on her jacket while Victor sat quietly, watching the departing guests carefully. "Yes, I think so," I said reluctantly, not relishing the thought of taking him back to his corner. "Tell you what. How about I give him a ride and you finish up the dishes?" I asked.

"Fair enough," he said, smiling.

I went out and found my jacket, and asked Victor, "You about ready?"

"Yeah, yeah. Should I change my clothes?" he queried.

"Tell you what, how about you keep those, and I'll take the others home, wash them, and bring them to you when you're ready for a change?"

He nodded approvingly. "Yeah, that sounds like a good idea."

"Want me to make you a to-go box in case you want a snack later?"

He smiled. "Good idea. But I'll see you tomorrow, right?"

"You bet, my friend."

Then I took him back to his corner. I was happy but sad at the same time. *What kind of hostess leaves her guest alone on a street corner in the dark, knowing he would be sleeping on the ground near a smelly dumpster behind the Sushi restaurant in a tattered sleeping bag all alone?* I thought. *So very alone.*

But he hopped out cheerfully with his box and cocoa. Smiling, he said, "Thanks for a great party. It was fun."

"I'm glad you were there, Victor. It's good to have my friends with me on my special day. See you tomorrow."

It was late by the time I dragged myself through the door. Dean had a cup of tea waiting for me as I changed my clothes and found my favorite pajamas. As we folded back the covers and crawled into our soft bed, he said, "Well, your friend certainly knows how to handle himself. Who would have ever thought that a guy that lives on the street would waltz in and act like nothing was out of the ordinary? It didn't seem to bother him at all," he said, then quietly asked, "So, how did it make you feel? Driving him back and leaving him?" Dean knew me very well.

"Horrible. I've seen where he sleeps. He seemed so grateful and happy to be included in the celebration. But really, I don't think I could feel more like an awful person right now. I'm sleeping with a soft pillow and he is huddled on the ground like a . . . a . . . well, a homeless person."

"Well, babe, that's what he is, you know."

"Yes, I know, but I don't like it. Surely there is something we can do?" I asked helplessly.

"Let's sleep on it, birthday girl. Tomorrow is another day. Just be happy it's not too cold or raining."

The next morning was Saturday, and I was so happy to have the rare opportunity to sleep in. I woke briefly to the sound of pounding rain on the metal patio roof and gratefully snuggled back under the covers. The house was quiet and dark; I was sleepy and cozy. As I lay there dozing, my mind drifted lazily over the prior evening, and all of a sudden I realized that while I was lying in my cozy bed, Victor was out in the rain! I bolted upright, sending the dog flying to the floor and uncovering Dean in the process. I leapt out of bed and turned on the light.

"What's happening? Did you hear a noise?" Dean sat up at my sudden movement.

"It's raining!" I exclaimed.

My husband stared at me with a sleepy, bemused expression. "Okay, good, rain is good. Now come back to bed. We don't have to go to work today."

Thumping his pillow, he pulled the covers up to his chin and settled back in place with a happy sigh. I hesitated for a moment and walked to the French doors to let the dog out, who, after taking a few steps, turned back to stare at me as if to say, "Are you kidding me?" Distracted, I shut the door in his face, his whining muffled by the rain beating heavily on the porch roof. I felt a cold breeze curl around my bare toes.

"Hey babe?" I sat down gingerly on his edge of the bed.

"Hmm?" he mumbled, eyes closed.

"Victor is out in the rain."

As I sat there, Dean remained still and quiet. I waited for him to respond. He finally opened one eye and peeked to see if I was still there. He closed his eye again, then sighed heavily. Inhaling a deep breath, he pushed himself to a sitting position. "And what exactly, my sweet wife, do you want me to do about that?" he asked, looking at me with a raised eyebrow.

"Well, it's really nasty. Can he come over just until the rain stops? I could dry out his clothes and he could just, I don't know, hang out and watch a movie or something?" As my voice rose up at the end in a hopeful question, I smiled sweetly with raised eyebrows as if to convey without words what a great idea it was. I waggled my eyebrows in a more exaggerated fashion and nodded vigorously. "What do you think?"

Dean burst out laughing.

"What's so funny?" I asked, feigning hurt.

"I can't believe you're sitting here on a great rainy Saturday morning, on your day off, telling me you want me to go out and collect a smelly homeless person from the corner and bring him to the house to hang out with us all day and watch movies. Who are you?"

"Well, I'm a girl that God got a hold of in a big way, and He tells me to love my neighbor as myself. And now my neighbor is out in the rain, and I can't enjoy my day if he is." I said sagely.

"And I suppose that since you won't be able to enjoy your day, I won't either. Is that a correct assessment?" he asked, wisely I might add.

"Yes, sir, that's a correct assessment." I smiled widely, knowing that his dismay was all a show. There is not a more tenderhearted man I know than Dean. "And, I even love you so much that I'll go get him, so you can stay in bed longer. How's that?" I asked extra syrupy sweet.

He sighed in feigned resignation. "I have a feeling sleep is out the window. How about I make some eggs and biscuits? That would be good on a cold morning. I bet he'll be hungry."

"Perfect!" I jumped up to get dressed. "I'll be back before you know it." I hurried back to the edge of the bed and gave his sweet face a loud smacking kiss. "I'll be right back with the package!" I laughed happily.

On my way out the door, I grabbed a few old towels and a bulky blanket. The streets were slick and the cars were sparse that early gray Saturday morning. It was two days before Christmas, and the only colors shining were the twinkling holiday lights decorating the light poles on Main Street. The rain continued to fall, and the wipers beat softly as the radio played Christmas carols in a happy tune. I pulled up across the street from Victor's corner and waited for the light to change. I could see him there in the clean clothes I had given him the previous night, standing in his customary spot in a large puddle. He had his hunched shoulders curled forward in the cold rain. I turned the corner and pulled into the parking lot as he turned to see who it was. He knelt down on the soaked grass and did his customary routine before approaching me. When he finally made it to my car, I rolled down my window and took in his soaked form.

"Hey friend. Wet out there?" I asked gently.

"Naw, naw, I'm alright," he said, through his quivering lips.

I cocked an eyebrow. "Really? You look kinda cold to me."

"I'm alright, alright."

That was enough for me. "Well, I'm not all right with you being outside. How about we go home?"

The question hung in the cold, damp air between us. He said nothing but stared at me with an unusually focused gaze. "Home?" he asked, with much emotion in the word.

"Yes, home. To my house. Let's dry out your clothes and hang out, watch some movies, maybe take a nap or two. Dean's there, he's making breakfast. What do you say?"

He held my gaze, his dark brown eyes bleak. Then, slowly, like a summer sunrise, his face relaxed. "Yeah, let's go home."

"Well, come on, what're you waiting for?"

I jumped out of the car in the steadily falling rain and went around to his side, spreading the towels over the leather seat. He climbed in oh-so-carefully so as not to get my Jeep dirty. I climbed in after him and noticed how stiffly he sat in his seat, with his arms straight out and hands carefully holding his knees. His hands were shaking badly. I reached over and patted his hands; they were icy cold. I cranked up the heat to high, then immediately had to open the window as he smelled so strongly of body odor. Nevertheless, off we went to the house. I was grateful that he was willing to leave the corner. I guess the misery of standing in the rain superseded his desire to wait for his mother that day. As we drove, he looked around with interest.

"Where you live?" he finally asked.

"Really close," I told him. "About fifteen minutes from your corner." We pulled into the driveway of our little twelve-hundred-square-foot house, which I refer to as our cozy bungalow. "Here you go! This is it!"

I pulled the Jeep into the garage and we exited the car. He was smelling so badly by this time that my first thought was to get him cleaned up before he sat on my furniture. "Tell you what, Victor, how about a nice hot shower to get you warmed up? I'll throw your clothes in the washer, and then we can have some breakfast. What do you think?"

He nodded slowly.

"Just leave your wet shoes out here on the porch. I'll wash them too."

He didn't look too happy about taking off his blue basketball shoes. "You going to give them back, right?" he asked a little suspiciously.

"Of course! Just a little cleanup," I promised.

He nodded and followed me inside. We headed across the tile floor to the bathroom, his sock-clad feet leaving huge, muddy prints on the floor.

Dean poked his head out from the kitchen. "Hey, Victor! You hungry?"

Victor looked up, then lifted his hand briefly in a small wave. "Yeah, yeah," he said, as he continued to trudge across the floor after me.

I got him situated with soap, towels, and shampoo, then left him to his own devices. I then wandered into the kitchen where Dean was cooking up a feast.

"So how did it go?" he asked right away.

"Well, I guess okay. He's not nearly as perky as he was last night. He seems tired. I assume there wasn't much sleeping in the rain."

We sat and chatted for what seemed like an hour while Victor enjoyed what was likely the longest shower of his life. He emerged in a cloud of steam, head still dripping wet down the back of Dean's too-small T-shirt. He sat at the table and wolfed down a huge meal of eggs and toast and orange juice. Afterward, I showed him to the couch and gave him the remote and a giant warm, fuzzy blanket. He asked if we had MTV. I said sure and spent a few minutes getting him situated. I sat with him, feeling somewhat awkward, but he didn't seem interested in conversation. A few minutes later I looked over and he was sound asleep, blanket clutched in one hand and the remote in the other. He slept for fourteen hours that day, never stirring. After Dean and I ate lunch, I did laundry, baked cookies, and cleaned; in all that time he never moved. Meanwhile, we went on about our day doing what we normally do on a rainy Saturday in December.

Later, as the rain continued to fall, we had a quiet conversation in the bedroom. Dean stated the obvious, "I guess he needs to stay here tonight. I watched the weather, and it's going to get colder and rain until early in the morning."

I nodded, grateful for his kindness, feeling I had asked too much already.

With Victor still not stirring, I didn't have the heart to wake him. Dean and I ate dinner, and I cleaned the kitchen, making Victor a plate so he could eat when he got up. I poked him gently and asked if he was hungry.

He said, "No, just tired," and sleepily agreed that he would be happy to spend the night.

So, we blew up our camping air mattress and placed it in the living room floor by the couch. After we piled on plenty of pillows and blankets, Victor immediately tried it out and declared it wonderfully comfortable, even though his feet hung way off the end. My little old dog, Henry, who hates everyone and embarrassingly enough is a biter, climbed right in next to Victor and curled up happily under the blankets.

Dean laughed. "Well, dogs are a good judge of character, so there you go. We know Victor is an all right guy."

The three of us, with hot chocolates, watched a marathon of Christmas movies, Dean and I on the couch and Victor on the air mattress, as rain pattered quietly on the roof. Around midnight we were watching *It's a Wonderful Life*. Toward the end of the movie, when the townspeople are singing "Auld Lang Syne" and the angel bell is ringing, I heard a scratchy voice. I looked down and there lay Victor, who had long been snoring before then, with his eyes closed, singing every word to the song.

As the angel bell was ringing in the movie, my tears began to flow. I knew we had done the right thing by bringing him to the house. I had no idea what would happen next or what we would even do the next day. But I knew the Lord was pleased.

CHAPTER 10

What Now?

As Dean and I bid Victor good night, he positively exuded con-tentment, lying there on the air mattress in the living room of our tiny bungalow, snuggled close to his pile of pillows and fuzzy blanket. We made sure he had everything he might need for the night before leaving him. It had been a long day; satisfying, although it was a little strange to have a street person sleeping on our living room floor.

I was pleased that Victor had spent the day inside and not out in the rain; nevertheless, the whole experience was a little disconcerting. Although I had been visiting him for months on the corner, this was the first time we had brought him into the house. Visiting someone is not the same as having them in your home and really knowing them. I wondered what would happen overnight. I knew Victor to be sweet and kind, but who knew what would happen when we were in bed? Would he rob us? Hurt us? Would he even be there in the morning? To say I did not think of these things would be painting an incomplete picture.

We locked our bedroom door, climbed into bed, pulled the

covers up to our chins, and just sort of lay there quietly. Then we looked at each other and burst into laughter. "Well, good night, see you in the morning?" Dean said with a smile and a wink. Oddly enough, we didn't talk about the thoughts rolling through our respective minds that night until months later. It just seemed unkind to express them out loud. But they were there between us, the proverbial elephant in the room. I slept lightly, listening for any little sound, unsure if I should unlock the door and check on him, even though his air mattress was just a mere six feet outside our door. We don't call it a cozy bungalow for nothing.

The next morning, Christmas Eve, was a Sunday. Church started at 9:00 a.m., so sleeping late was out of the question, even though my light sleep had left me feeling tired. Dean was still asleep, and I saw that it was still raining and cold when I let the dogs out. I unlocked the bedroom door to check on our guest. He was still asleep as well. It didn't look like he had moved all night. I realized at that moment how exhausted he must have been.

I left him there and went into the kitchen to make coffee and contemplate the day. I had not thought about it, but since we were headed to church in just over an hour, what were we going to do with Victor? All my clattering about did not bring so much as a glimmer of wakefulness from our houseguest, so I took my coffee with me to the bedroom and sat down on the same spot as yesterday, the edge of the mattress on Dean's side. I sat quietly sipping as Dean rolled over and threw his arm over his eyes.

"Yes?" he queried. "What is it today?"

I grinned into my cup. "I brought you a cup of coffee because I like you so much."

He sniffed. "I'm not buying it." He was not to be fooled. "What's up with your friend out there? He still here?"

"Yes. As a matter of fact, he's still here, snoring happily.

Question, though, what are we going to do with him when we go to church? I mean, I'll ask him if he wants to go with us, but if not, then what? Can we leave him here by himself? What's the protocol here?"

Dean uncovered his eyes. "Oh, I didn't think about that. Well, not really. I'm not sure I'm comfortable leaving him here in the house alone. We don't know him *that* well."

"Ugh, okay, that's what I thought too. Here's what sucks, it's still raining."

"Well, it's only seven thirty, maybe it'll quit before we have to go." He raised his eyebrows and lifted his shoulders in indecision.

Needless to say, after I had woken Victor and fed him a hearty breakfast, it was still raining. The fact that it was Christmas Eve and the heavy downpour was still in full swing made the thought of returning him to the corner even worse. Honestly, we had not thought this all the way through. I asked Victor how he felt about going to a shelter or a hotel. "Naw, naw, I'm alright, you can take me back to the corner, I'll be fine."

I spent twenty minutes explaining to him that it was cold and raining, and asking, "Are you sure you don't want to go to church with us? Are you sure there's no one else who would like to have you over for the day?" But he was firm. It was the corner and nothing else. No amount of persuading on my part would get him to agree to go anywhere else. I let it drop. I gave him his clean, dry clothes and found extra socks, a scarf, gloves, and a hat for him.

Dean and I dressed for church in silence; neither of us was feeling good about taking him back to the corner, but we were also uncomfortable leaving him unattended in our home. The three of us walked to the Jeep in silence. The windshield wipers seemed especially loud in the quiet of the car.

As we pulled into the parking lot, I twisted in my seat and

said, "Victor, please let us take you to the hotel. There is one literally across the street. You could look out the window and see the corner from there!"

He was adamant. "No, I want to stay here."

We stopped the car by the awning of the building nearest to the corner and pointed out that there was a bench there, out of the wind and rain. Victor said nothing as he opened the door and stepped out into the steady drizzle. He assured us that he would be fine. He rejected the raincoat, boots, and umbrella I had loaded into the car. It broke my heart to think of leaving him there alone on Christmas Eve, but I really did not know what else to do with him. Dean shook his hand by the car door and resumed his spot in the driver's seat. I stood there helplessly, in the cold, wet rain with Victor. He stood very still as I pulled the stocking cap firmly down over his ears and to his eyebrows, turned up the collar of his jacket, tucked in the ends of the scarf around his thin neck, and pulled the sleeves down firmly.

The cold wind was as cutting as a knife as I turned back to the Jeep. When I opened the door and leaped into my seat, the wind brought in a wash of blowing rain. I pulled the door closed behind me, grateful for the heater blowing full blast. I sat there wiping at my face with the edge of my scarf. The rain began to pelt the top of the Jeep relentlessly. The heater blowing full blast was causing the windows to fog as I sat there trying not to look at him. I pulled my sweater over my hand and scrubbed at the inside of the windshield. He was just standing there in the parking lot, the wind blowing rain sideways through the dim morning.

"Are you kidding me with this?" Dean turned to me incredulously. "He's really going to stand there in the rain? I thought when he saw how bad the weather is he would change his mind! You told him we would take him to a hotel, right?"

"I did, but I can't force him to do what I want him to do," I said resignedly.

Victor's eyes met mine through the foggy windshield that morning. His face completely impassive, no emotion whatsoever, just looking at me. The rain was dripping from his chin and his fingertips. I knew his fingers must be cold, but they hung straight down to his side. I clenched mine together as if somehow it would warm his. He was wearing his Carhartt jumpsuit that would soon be soaked through. I had washed it, but it still stank of body odor and sweat. He stood straight and still, tall as an oak tree, in dank, wet cold.

Dean put the Jeep in reverse and began to back away slowly. Victor lifted one dripping wet hand slowly, shoulder high. Not even a wave, just a resigned acknowledgment that we were leaving him there. We continued to back away as the first tear slowly began to creep its way down my face. The lights from the high beams caught him one last time as we turned around and sat waiting to exit the parking lot. The car idled for a few long moments. I glanced at Dean, his jaw was clenched and his fingers were tightly gripping the steering wheel. In the side mirror I could see Victor standing there still watching us. It felt so wrong to leave him there, and yet neither of us knew what to do that morning.

I could not have felt more like a hypocrite when I stepped into the warm, inviting church service a few minutes later. Families sat snugly shoulder to shoulder, and greetings were called out as arms were thrown around old friends and smiles were warmly exchanged. As the congregation sang Christmas carols, read Scripture, and lighted candles, I mulled over the situation facing me. The verse that continued to roll through my mind during that service on Christmas Eve was Proverbs 31:20: "She opens her hand to the poor and reaches out her hands to the needy" (ESV).

The woman described in Proverbs 31 is a blessing to everyone around her. Her family, her friends, and even her town are blessed, because of all that she does to lead and serve those around her. One of her remarkable characteristics this verse speaks of is how she generously extends a hand of compassion and helps the poor. Oh, how it resonated with me on that eve of the birth of this Savior of mine. Yeah, I had reached out my hand to the poor all right. Then I threw him back out on the street.

We were celebrating the birth of a King. I knew as I sat there among my fellow brothers and sisters in Christ that the baby who was born in the manger was who He said He was. I knew He changed lives, and I knew He was calling me. Had it been an audible voice, it could not have been any clearer. For weeks I had been praying that God would send someone to help Victor, and He sent me. I could not avoid it any longer. If I had the love and appreciation for this Christ I served as I claimed, the One who came to the earth and served man, He was letting me know it was now time for me to serve Him, to wash feet as He had done. I was slowly beginning to understand this burning passion. I reminded myself of the hardships, hunger, and beatings many of the disciples of Christ endured for their passion.

Dean and I had a difficult conversation on the way home. He felt a tremendous amount of empathy for Victor, just as I did. Yet we were both so unsure of what to do about it. We had planned a dinner that evening with our extended family, and bringing Victor along just didn't seem like something we should impose on the holiday celebration. I thought of asking Dean if it was okay for me to skip it to take care of Victor, but not spending the evening with the family didn't seem like a good option either. I was frustrated that I didn't know what helping Victor looked like. All the options were lacking as far as I could see.

I did not say much as we continued about our day. The kids were home, and I was in the kitchen baking for tomorrow's Christmas feast. Nicki, happy to be home from college, was wrapped in a blanket in front of the fireplace, while her younger brother, Aaron (taller than his big sister now), hung out in the kitchen as he always did when sweets were involved, "helping" by licking the beaters and keeping me company just like he had when he was a little boy. I told him what was going on with Victor, and we discussed what we should do next. He was not impressed that we had taken him back to the corner.

"Are you kidding, Mom? You just left him standing there in the rain? That's harsh!" he reminded us. "Why don't you start a Facebook page? Lots of people drive by there every day. Maybe someone knows his mom, or someone might have an idea on how to help him. Better yet, set up a GoFundMe account and raise some money to get him a room and some clothes!"

He thought it was a great idea, and before I had a moment to absorb what all of this might mean, he leapt up to grab his laptop and busily began to type, shoving a forgotten warm cookie to the side to create a workspace for himself. As he worked I said a silent prayer of thanks. Sometimes the Lord gives such direct confirmation.

For several weeks I had been praying and mulling over the idea of creating a Facebook page to reach out to anyone who might have some ideas about what we could do. I had honestly held off for this long because I had Matthew 6:1 rolling around in my mind: "Be careful not to practice your righteousness in front of others to be seen by them. If you do, you will have no reward from your Father in heaven." But that day I knew the Lord was leading me to step out, and I felt confident with this decision, based on prayer. This had nothing to do with me or with me thinking I was some sort of saving "angel" and seeking to have others pat me on the back. This was about helping Victor.

Within ten minutes Aaron announced, "Mom, here you go, write up something really good. Tell the story and put a good picture of Victor on there." He grabbed the mixing spoon from my hand and pushed me toward the table, taking a big bite of dough on the way to the bowl. He proceeded to dump, add, and stir ingredients while I sat there, unsure of what to do with all this, and frankly overwhelmed.

"Well, wait Aaron, let's think this through for a minute. What if he doesn't want to be on Facebook? What if no one gives any money? Who is responsible for the money? I don't know anything about GoFundMe . . ."

"Oh, come on, Mom. Do you want to help him or not?"

Well, goodness, who am I to argue with the logic of a teenager on a mission? It meant a lot to me that Aaron was interested in helping Victor. Reaching out and helping someone else was foreign to me. I was always much more in the "let's wait for someone else to take care of it" camp, and then criticizing as they did it. I figured the worst thing that could happen is that no one would donate, so what harm was there? I spent the next twenty minutes or so writing down what I knew of Victor's story for the GoFundMe page, with Aaron tweaking here and there, adding details. We high-fived over our final draft:

> Victor is born of a beautiful soul that stands on the corner of El Camino Real and Nasa Road 1 in Clear Lake, Texas. Hundreds of people drive past him every week and wonder

> what in the world his story might be. . . . He stands and looks, taps the pole, squints, dances, waves, and sometimes just stares. He is a sweet, gentle man that needs our help. If you have ever heard the term "falling through the cracks," he is the definition. Police, fire, and local city mental health resources know of him. Know him very well, in fact. It is said that his mother dropped him on the corner and told him to wait for her to come back. He believed her. So, he waits, and waits, and waits. We, as a community, are coming together to find him the help he needs. That is priority one. Once we get him stable in that regard, it is my desire to see him in a peaceful home with friends to support him, and perhaps even a job. If you want to meet someone who is eternally optimistic, positive, and humble, go visit him. He will out-bless you every time.

The only thing left to do was to name the page. My fingers sat poised above the keyboard as I thought about our community. So many people knew him by sight, but few knew his name. It seemed only logical when I typed, "This Is Victor." Aaron was scraping the last of the cookie dough from the bowl. The good smells emanating from the oven brought Dean sauntering into the room to see what goodies he could relieve us of.

"Hey, Dean, we're making Victor a Facebook page and GoFundMe," Aaron said.

"Hmfph?" With raised eyebrows, Dean turned around, a cookie in each hand and a mouth full. He swallowed quickly. "GoFundMe? What for?"

"To help Victor," said Aaron matter-of-factly.

I laughed at Dean's surprised expression. "It makes me feel better," I said. "I'm still sad we left him on the corner this morning. Do you think I can go get him tomorrow? He shouldn't be out there on Christmas by himself."

"Um, okay, and yes?" Dean said quizzically. "I was in the other room only for an hour and you guys decided all this?"

"Well, I figure if we get a few hundred people to at least see this thing, maybe someone will have a good idea about what the next step should be. I've done all the research, remember. As far as I can tell, we have no shelter here, not that he would go anyways. And he really needs to see a doctor, seeing as how some days he doesn't even make sense, and standing there on the corner rain or shine is not exactly rational."

"True," Dean agreed. "Be interesting to see what people come up with." After grabbing a few more cookies and a glass of milk, he disappeared into the living room.

I hesitated, tapping on the computer for few more minutes. Finally, with "Okay, done," I hit Submit. It was Christmas Eve 2016, and "This Is Victor" went live on Facebook and GoFundMe. I also shared the page on my personal and business Facebook pages, then closed the laptop with a snap.

"Time for my cookies." I smiled at Aaron. We toasted with tall glasses of milk, then went in search of Dean and *Rudolph the Red-Nosed Reindeer.*

Christmas was no longer like I remembered when the kids were little and they would leap into bed to wake Ben and me at 5:00 a.m., desperate to open the gifts piled under the twinkling lights of the tall Christmas tree. I even slept in, waking up later than usual. I plugged in the Christmas tree on my way to the kitchen and smiled at Aaron sleeping on the couch wrapped in blankets with his dog, Daisy, who peeked at me before tucking her head back under the covers.

I read my Bible that morning at the kitchen table, with coffee in my favorite mug. My early morning time with the Lord is especially precious, and I lingered over it that day with a grateful heart and many prayers for those I loved, and of course, for Victor on the corner. I knew he would be in his usual spot that morning, and as I kneaded dough for homemade sticky buns, I made sure to double the recipe to share with our new friend.

Eventually Nicki and Dean rolled out of their respective rooms to greet the day, less anxious for presents than they were for breakfast. And Aaron came to the table, still wrapped in his blanket. Gifts aside, I think it was likely the smell of bacon that brought them to the kitchen that morning. After breakfast the kids retreated for a post-breakfast nap, and I sat down to talk with Dean over a second cup of coffee.

"Do you have a plan for Victor yet?" he asked.

"Today or for the rest of his life?" I laughed.

"Yeah," he said, agreeing as he opened the laptop in front of him. "That definitely needs clarification. I know you and I—" He stopped speaking and stared at the screen in front of him. "Have you looked at his Facebook page?"

"No," I answered, concerned. "What's wrong?"

Shaking his head, he turned the screen around to me. "You have five thousand people who liked the page."

My head snapped back in surprise as I stared at the screen. "What? I thought at most a couple of hundred."

"Looks like there are way more people than you who are concerned about him!" Dean said, smiling.

About that time, I heard Aaron yell, "*Mom!*" from the hallway. He quickly rounded the corner to the kitchen at a gallop.

"Did you see the GoFundMe? There's almost eight thousand dollars in the account! We're going to be able to help Victor! How cool is that for a Christmas gift?" He was beaming. We all were. The outpouring of love and compassion from our community was overwhelming.

I was stunned by the sweet comments and concern from people all over the city. As the day progressed, the likes, shares, and comments continued to roll in, as well as the funds to the account, which was growing by the hour. There were dozens of messages from people offering thoughts, ideas, and donations.

Even my sweet elderly neighbor down the street knocked on my door that morning with bags of gifts for Victor: a shaving kit, brand-new clothes, even slippers and a pair of tennis shoes. Her generosity and thoughtfulness were just a taste of the outpouring to come over the next few weeks. By lunchtime that Christmas Day, my living room looked more like a thrift shop than a home. I stood worried amidst the boxes and bags of clothing, food, gift cards, toiletries, and books.

"Where in the world am I going to put all this stuff?" I wondered aloud.

Dean began to laugh. "This has been the most interesting Christmas I've ever experienced. God sure showed up in the hands and feet of all of *our* neighbors, didn't He?"

I met his eyes. "Yes, He did. He's just good that way. I'm going to get Victor and bring him over so he can open all his gifts. He's going to be like a kid in a candy store!"

Less than an hour later I stood on the corner with Victor. To my surprise, I was in the midst of yet another mountain of gifts and wrapping paper blowing in the wind. People who had seen his page brought him gifts at his corner that morning. Victor was dancing around, laughing and pointing. "Look at this one!

A watch! And it's blue! My favorite color! I even have shoes, and pants, and shirts!" He picked up one item after another, only to excitedly drop it back in the dirt to pick up the next one. "I've had friends over all morning! So many people came to see me and hug me! What a great day!"

I was quickly picking up after him, not really sure what to do with all the gifts. Where in the world do people who live on the streets keep all their stuff? It's not like Victor had a closet to hang his clothes or a dresser to store anything. But one thing was clear: people cared, and they cared a lot. There were many willing and able to help, and I was not in this alone.

After celebrating at Victor's corner, I began to load the car. But Victor was too excited to help. He was zinging from the light pole to the car, to the curb, and back again like a child on sugar overload. I managed to corral everything into the car, including Victor, then cracked the window open to bring some freshness to his ever-present fragrance.

At the house he plowed through the mountain of gifts from more well-wishers, our own presents left mostly forgotten under the tree. Reveling in the light radiating from his face, the gifts the family had purchased for each other seemed pale in comparison.

A beautiful custom bicycle from a local bike shop and a donated cell phone were his favorites. The cell phone was a standard flip phone, but he was enamored by the idea of being able to call his mother. He was so excited, in fact, that I didn't have the heart to tell him we had no idea what her phone number was. After a plate of sticky buns and a big glass of orange juice, he finally succumbed to exhaustion and fell asleep among the wrapping papers; he was upright, propped against the couch pillows, with an unopened gift on his lap and a smile on his face.

With Victor napping happily on the couch in "his spot," as he had called it earlier that day, we quietly opened our gifts. We discussed what to do with his Christmas gifts and decided that the least we could do was to give him a clean change of clothes daily, and to make sure he did not have anything with him on the corner that would be of interest to someone who might want to relieve him of his gifts. We took him back to the corner later that day.

In the following days, we would pick him up as time allowed and invite him to come over for a few hours for lunch or dinner. I stopped by every day to check on him while messages and phone calls poured in daily and the Facebook page and the GoFundMe account continued to grow. People were stopping by the corner to shake his hand, and he was flush with Subway sandwiches and hot cocoa.

I received messages and running commentary from people I didn't even know about what was happening on the corner when I wasn't there. The entire community was looking out for him in the spirit of the holiday season. I was completely overwhelmed and spent the better part of my days speaking with people who offered insight and help, making notes, and working with the community to come up with a workable solution. Since it was the week between Christmas and New Year's, my business was closed, but so were the governmental agencies that could help Victor.

CHAPTER 11

New Year and Good-Bye Corner

The week after Christmas, Houston temperatures plummeted. The morning of New Year's Day, I stood on the corner with Victor and his fresh, clean Carhartt jumper in my hand, still warm from the dryer, and hot chocolate cooling in my car. I was bent double, holding the leg of Victor's jumper as he hopped about on one foot with his hand on top of my head for balance, attempting to hit the leg hole of the jumper with his Nike-clad foot. I was cold, grumpy, and tired. I stood up straight as he continued to hop and, folding the jumper over my arm, I said with an edge to my voice, sternly looking him right in the eye, "Victor, I'm done with this."

"What you mean?" He stopped hopping, long arms dangling down by his sides.

"This is ridiculous. It's freezing cold out here and it's probably going to rain tonight. I'm done with you hanging out here in the cold and sleeping on the ground. It's time for you to be inside. I'm not taking no for an answer." I crossed my arms and stood still, ready for a disagreement.

A passing car slowed down and honked loudly. "Hey, Victor!" someone yelled out the window. Victor raised his hand in a happy wave and turned back to me.

"I can't go to a hotel," he argued. Gesturing to the passing car, he continued, "My friends won't be able to find me. My mom won't be able to find me."

I could see he was enjoying the attention and his newfound fame. "I will put a message on Facebook for all the world to see. My mind is made up. We are going to a hotel. Today. Time to get in the car."

Apparently, my authority and stern voice did the trick. Or it was the fact that it was miserably cold that finally trumped his desire to be outside. We turned from the corner that day, shoulder to shoulder, and walked to the car. I hoped never to stand there on that corner again.

I called Dean and gave him the news. "Finally!" he exclaimed. "I'll be right there."

He met Victor and me at the Motel 6 across the street from Victor's corner. We waited in the car while Dean went inside, but moments later he came out looking disconcerted. As he climbed in the truck, he asked Victor, "Have you ever stayed here before?"

"Yeah, one time a nice guy paid for me to stay here two nights," he replied.

"Right, that's what they told me. I think we better try the hotel next door. This might not be the perfect spot." He raised his eyebrows at me meaningfully. Later he told me the clerk said the room was in a horrible mess during Victor's stay, and he had been asked to leave.

I said nothing, and Victor, too, was quiet in the back seat.

Thankfully, at the next hotel the front desk clerk knew exactly who Victor was and didn't mind him staying there. She sweetly gave us a weekly discount and a large corner room that was off to the side with an outside door, away from the main flow of guests. She reassured us she was delighted to see Victor indoors and would personally keep an eye on him and help him with anything he might need.

We took the key card and presented it to Victor in a grand gesture, but he looked scared and unsure there in the back seat. His thin shoulders hunched forward as he held himself and rocked back and forth. I stood outside the car in the biting wind and held out my hand. "Come on, my friend, let's go see your new room."

We followed Dean around the car and up the sidewalk. He opened the door with a flourish and flicked on the light switch. The overly warm, stale air assaulted our nostrils as we stepped inside. I sucked in my breath and quickly glanced at Dean as he did the same. Nonetheless, we forged on. Victor stepped tentatively over the threshold, looked around, and said in a wonder-filled voice, "Wow, I have my own couch!" He stepped forward quickly and began to explore the new room. In addition to a couch, he was thrilled with his coffee table, mini fridge, and king-sized bed. I knew then that it was going to be all right.

"Tell you what, why don't I run into the store and get you a few things for your mini fridge?" I asked.

"Yeah! How about some frozen burritos and some orange juice?"

"That sounds great," I replied.

After a trip to the store, we got Victor situated. I made sure he had his toothbrush and toiletries, then it was time for Dean and me to go home for the night. I wondered if Victor would stay in the room or walk back to the familiarity of the corner. Maybe he wondered that himself.

With my hand on the doorknob, I looked at him. He stood in the middle of the room, suddenly looking lost. "Cheer up, my friend, I'll be here in the morning. Then I'll take you to the dining room and show you how to use the waffle machine."

He perked up quickly, a smile forming at the corner of his downturned mouth. "Yeah, I'd like that. Waffles are good. One other thing though. Do you think that you could bring some air freshener when you come back? This room doesn't smell real fresh."

I swallowed my laughter. "Of course, Victor, I would be happy to get you some air freshener."

I closed the door quietly behind me, breathing a prayer of thankfulness. "I think he's going to be okay," I told Dean.

"Me too," Dean laughed. "Just as soon as we take care of that smelly room."

I punched him playfully. "Let's go home. For once since I met Victor, I might actually get a good night's sleep!"

Thankfully, one of the many messages I had received was from the Webster fire chief. Chief Shipp and his men had watched over Victor for years, and they had fed and clothed him many times as well as checked on him on the corner. But much like the other agencies in town, they could only do so much. So Chief Shipp had made it his personal mission to take care of Victor to the best of his professional ability.

He told me the story of Victor wandering into the fire house bay one day and getting "trapped," if you will, seemingly unable to find the exit. Victor walked from corner to corner, touching all the poles and becoming increasingly agitated. He was stuck there until one of the firemen kindly pointed him toward the door, where he was able to find his way back to the corner.

When I shared with him my limited access to Victor's medical history because I was not a family member, he made calls to the county health officials in his capacity as fire chief. Because he was considered a medical professional, he was granted access to Victor's health records. He was able to step in and smoothly turn the wheels that had ground to a frustrating halt.

After reading his records and diagnosis, Chief Shipp and I sat together with Victor to discuss his health. We explained to him the steps he would have to take to relieve some of the more difficult aspects of his medical issues. The most important one, a nonnegotiable, was taking his medication daily. The symptoms that had held Victor captive for so many years could be controlled with just a small amount of this medication. Thankfully, Victor was agreeable. Our story would be vastly different had he not made the decision to allow us to help him.

I also took the chief up on his offer to make sure that Victor was tucked safely in his bed each night. He reassured me that every evening the firefighters would go by the hotel and do a well check on Victor. Dean and I were anxious to see if Victor would indeed stay on his medication, as well as stay in his room.

Victor was always happy to have company, and I was glad to find him very cheerful in general. I knew by now that I was firmly committed to Victor, but I also knew that in the past I had jumped into projects only to realize later that I had overcommitted. I was also concerned about Victor's feelings. I didn't want him to become attached to me if somehow in the future I was going to let him down. Thoughts of how I had walked away from my own children lay heavy in my heart. I was determined not to make the same mistake, but I had learned long ago to never say never. This was big. Victor had too many people in his life walk away from him already, and I did not want to become another one.

I pressed forward in my quest to untangle the web of governmental bureaucracy that hindered my obtaining identification for this kind man. Victor could not remember the last time he had an ID card or any other formal documentation. Without an ID, though, there would be no disability benefits or health insurance, and no possibility of a bank account or any type of employment in the future.

In an endless circle of phone calls, I hit dead ends. I couldn't access important information because I was not related to him. Yet he was not capable of making these calls himself. Every spare moment I had was spent emailing or making phone calls. There was such a dizzying amount of communication with so many governmental agencies that, in addition to my work and family, Victor's needs were, frankly, overwhelming.

Many times, as I sat on hold yet again, I would doodle on my thick binder filled with "Victor" information—drawings, pictures, and my kids' names in bubble letters surrounded by hearts. My children were never far from my mind. I thought a lot about the motherly instinct inside me that was so concerned about Victor being hurt. Where had that been when I left Ben? My kids still deal with the consequences of my absence from their lives when they needed me the most.

I couldn't shake the feeling that God was giving me an opportunity to walk out my faith. I knew I was forgiven, but by serving Victor, I hoped to show Him that He had truly changed me and made me a new person. This was personal growth, sanctification, the act of becoming holy. It's God's will for us who call Him Lord. It says in 1 Thessalonians 4:7, "God has called us to live holy lives, not impure lives" (NLT). To sanctify something is to set it apart for special use; to sanctify a person is to make them holy. Jesus said a lot about that in John 17:16–17: "They are not of the world, even as I am not of it. Sanctify them by the truth; your word is truth."

In those weeks and months, people from my community and from across the country continued to call and send messages. It is not an exaggeration to say that the situation with Victor quickly overtook everything in my life. I still prayed, still sat and spent time with the Lord, but I know now that my eyes had left Him in those first months of the new year. They were often fixed on the situation before me rather than on Him. Over the roar of the other voices in my ears, the still, soft voice of Him had grown dim. I wanted it to be about how God works, His redemption, His might, His glory, His working through others; about the Lord allowing me to participate in His service to be His hands and feet as He lifted Victor from his situation, much in the same way by His grace I had been redeemed from mine. But the voices of the busyness of my life were ringing loudly.

The distractions muddied the waters and took the focus off

God. It would have been easier had I been focused on Him. That was a hard lesson to learn. Just as in my first marriage when I had made the decision to leave, and then to divorce, God's voice was becoming lost in my decision making. One thing I now know, by bitter experience, is that not asking God for guidance and wisdom is extremely unwise.

CHAPTER 12

You Don't Scare Me

Victor was adamant that he did not want help from Social Services. In his mind that was for disabled people, and he assured me he was not disabled. He vehemently informed me on many occasions that he stood on the corner because that was where he wanted to be.

He felt anger at the words I knew must have been spoken to him in his past. I did everything I could to assure him that Social Services wasn't for people who were messed up or broken in any way. I explained that we all need help sometimes, and that we need to help each other. Then I would continue my quest, deciding to deal with the fallout of his anger later. In one breath he would be upset over Social Security benefits, and in the next I would see him eating waffles, dripping syrup from his hands. The incongruity of his thoughts and behaviors was always perplexing to me. He was so astute about many things, but in others he was like a small child.

I came to realize that he was ten years behind in terms of current events. My first clue was when he asked to watch MTV, which had been at the height of popularity in the 1980s. The first time I spoke to him about his Facebook page, he had no idea what it was. He would talk about liking computers and then say something about saving to a floppy disk. He also asked me one day to buy him a Walkman with headphones, not understanding this was virtually a thing of the past. The pop culture and TV shows he watched were all old-school. And although he was thirty-three and could tell you how old he was, his mind seemed frozen in his early twenties.

The dizzying amount of change he was experiencing was very stressful for him. But he embraced it cheerfully. Occasionally, his brow would furrow when I would explain what a memory stick was or how an email worked. Many days I would nearly give up, frustrated that he couldn't understand what I was describing. I would throw up my hands in frustration, only to have Aaron come behind me and explain it flawlessly, after which Victor would pat me on the shoulder and tell me in a very serious tone, "It's alright, I just need a young person to help me out."

I would roll my eyes and laugh. "Well, thank goodness you have someone here your own age."

He would nod wisely.

He spent hours combing Facebook, reading comments, and taking much cheer from his "friends," although his friends were only a reminder that he was lonely. His solution was to migrate back to the corner daily to see them, sending me into a panic many evenings when I couldn't find him in his hotel room. I alerted the fire department that when they did their nightly check, they might want to run by the corner first before heading to the hotel.

One particular night Chief Shipp called and said, "I don't

know what to tell you. We looked in all of the usual spots and he's just not to be found." I feared the worst, that perhaps he had disappeared completely or had gone to see one of his old "friends" from the corner. He had told me many stories over the last months that made me cringe, most recently about a friend named Delores.

According to Victor, she lived in a neighborhood a "skateboard ride" away from the corner. He told me he had lived with her for a while at one point, but he did not know how long ago that was. I suspected from the nature of our last conversation that this was where he had gone.

Giving up on finding him now that it was dark, I spent the night hours tossing and turning, prayerfully talking it over with God, trying not to wake Dean. Checking my phone and rechecking, I thought about so many people who had homeless or drug-addicted family members and even children. What a heartbreaking roller-coaster ride of emotion life becomes when you care for a person who is unstable.

In the early morning, after checking my messages and seeing nothing from him, I began calling his phone every thirty minutes. It wasn't like him to not answer me. Eventually, about 11:00 a.m. my phone rang. I snatched it up quickly and said very nonchalantly, "Hello, this is Pizza Hut. Can I take your order?" I learned that he had indeed ridden his bicycle to her house and stayed the night. But now, in the cold light of morning, she was angry. He would not tell me why, other than to say that she was "just acting crazy," and asked if I could pick him up.

"Of course," was my response. "Where exactly are you?"

His hand covered the phone and I heard him, muffled, asking for the address. Then I heard a loud response even through the hand-covered phone. "Do not tell anyone where I live!"

He returned to our conversation and said, "Oh, never mind,

I'm fine. I'll see you later." He hung up quickly before I had the chance to respond.

I held the phone out and looked blankly at the black screen. What just happened here? This did not sound good. Every hair on the back of my neck stood up straight, and I quickly called Victor's number. It went directly to voice mail. *Oh no, you don't, lady.* I did not know her any more than by a name and a few stories from Victor, but I knew enough to realize she was bad news. I jumped up from my desk in my home office and ran into the bedroom to find my shoes as Dean was getting ready to walk out the door.

"Where's the fire?" he asked me. I quickly told him what was happening while hopping about putting on my tennis shoes and quickly pulling my hair into a high ponytail. "Hold up there, lady," Dean said. Laying a calm hand on my arm, he stopped me mid-hop and asked, "Where are you going? I thought you just said he didn't give you the address?"

I threw my hands in the air, knocking his hand away. "He didn't. But I don't care. I know he's somewhere within a bike ride from his corner. I'm going to head that way and keep calling him. Maybe he'll pick up and I'll be nearby. If nothing else, I know her name, and I'll go to the police station if I have to!"

"Okay, calm down. I'm sure he's fine. He knew this person way before you ever picked him up off the street." This man, always the voice of reason. "Do you want me to go with you?"

I grabbed him in a smothering hug. *I love this guy. Willing to dump his whole morning of appointments to drive all over town looking for Victor. Oh, he would be doing it for me, but he, too, has a soft, protective place in his heart for our gentle giant.* "No, I'm fine, but if I need you I'll call, and I'll definitely let you know when I get him back."

"I know you will. Be careful," he cautioned.

A quick peck on the cheek, and I was grabbing my purse and dialing Victor's number with one hand as I hurried to my car. Straight to voice mail again. As I backed down the driveway, I decided to head toward the corner where Victor had stood for so long. I figured that would be as good a place as any to start. As I drove and continued to dial, I began to pray that I would find him, that he would be okay, that God would take this person out of his life. I thought about how easily Victor trusted people. He possessed a sweet innocence and lack of understanding that attracted those who would take advantage of him with no regard. I knew in the depths of my soul that this lady was one of them, and I was determined that she understand in no uncertain terms that her time in Victor's life was now over.

As I was approaching his corner, the phone finally rang. It was Victor. I kept my voice light as though nothing was wrong. "Hey, my friend, what you up to?"

"Oh, nothing." He sounded anxious. "I just wanted you to know I'm alright."

"Of course, I know you're all right. You're a grown-up, right? I'm not worried about you." I added brightly, "Hey, what did you have for breakfast?" The one thing I know about Victor is that he rarely refuses a meal.

"Breakfast?" he answered quizzically.

"Yes, breakfast." I pulled over into the nearest parking lot and strained to hear any talking in the background. "What did you have for breakfast? I had toast and coffee, same as always."

"Uh," he stammered, never a good sign. "I didn't eat. I'll get something."

"You didn't eat? Well, you are at your friend's house, right? A good hostess always feeds her guests."

"Oh, I don't know. I don't think there's any food here. I'll go see."

"No!" I nearly yelled. I took a deep breath, then asked, "Hey, why don't I bring you a nice, hot McDonald's cheeseburger and some crispy, crunchy fries? I'll even get you a Victor special tri-colored shake." I let that carrot dangle in the silence for a few minutes.

His voice came back, quiet this time. "She won't tell me the address."

"Well, silly," I said, in a forced cheerful tone. "Go outside and look on the house. I bet if you think about it you know what street it is, don't you?" I knew I needed to tread lightly and not be too pushy. He was so nervous, I was afraid he would hang up again.

"What's happening here, my lovey?" I heard a loud voice. I winced. Delores had appeared as he tried to walk outside. I heard a sharp scuffle and then a syrupy sweet voice came over the line. "How do you do, Miss Ginger? I got quite an earful about you last night. How are you on this beautiful day?" she simpered into the mouthpiece.

I kept my voice equally sweet, gripping the steering wheel tightly. "I'm just wonderful, Miss Delores. I know you have Victor over there, and he's hungry. I know how much it takes to feed him. I'm on my way to run some errands, so I thought I would swing by and drop off a burger for him and be on my way, you know, to make things easier for you."

"Why, what a lovely thought from such a lovely lady." Her voice had now taken on the accent of a genteel Southern belle, a really creepy one. This change in her voice made me uneasy. I felt the urgency of getting Victor out of her house as soon as possible.

"I can only imagine how busy you must be, especially having

guests in the house," I tried again. "Popping by would be no problem at all."

Holding my breath, I waited for the response. A Texas twang this time. "Ah right, honey, what a selfless doll you are," she drawled into the phone. "Sure, here is the address. We look forward to seeing y'all real soon."

Is she kidding with this? I wondered. The accents were in the extreme. Maybe she was mocking me? But, regardless, armed with the address, I hit the nearest McDonald's and headed her way.

I had expected a run-down neighborhood and was shocked by the normal scene around me as I drove down her street. I parked in the driveway and stopped for a moment. I was determined not to leave without Victor, come hell or high water. I hesitated for a moment more, then sent a quick text to Dean to let him know where I was, knowing he would tell me it was a bad idea. I felt squeamish almost, her behavior on the phone sending so many red flags waving that an angry bull would have given pause for thought.

As I opened the door of the Jeep to step out, I looked around the front yard. At first glance the house and yard were tidy, but as I approached the front porch, I saw cigarette butts in abundance, two bicycles stuffed haphazardly in the bushes, and trash and papers strewn about the flower bed. More concerning, though, was an older African American man who looked to be in his sixties. He was crouched in the corner by the front door on his haunches, rocking slightly and humming.

"Hi, is this Delores's house?" I asked.

The question seemed inane as he was obviously in no condition to answer me. He paused his humming briefly, let out a "Humph," and his vacant, haunting eyes met mine. Then suddenly he smiled, a giant toothless grin. He again said, "Humph," and then immediately went back to his rocking and humming. I resisted the urge to turn and run back to the car.

The porch was on the small side and crowded with chairs, dead houseplants, and a bench. I took a step farther and jumped as a tall, lean man I recognized as homeless from around town rode up on another bicycle. Dismounting, he threw it angrily on its side in the grass and stomped past me. I don't think he even realized I was there. He continued ahead of me to the front door and threw it open with a bang, disappearing inside and leaving it open. The man in the corner didn't take any notice of his sudden appearance. I hesitantly approached the door and peered inside.

"Hello?" I called out, not too loudly, not wanting the angry man to come back to the door. The smell of body odor and rank old food assaulted my nostrils, so I thought better of walking in. Instead, I leaned out a bit to push the doorbell, hoping against hope that Victor would come to the door and I could grab him and run. I waited. Then, leaning over to the silent sidekick, I asked, "Nice day, huh?"

No response this time.

The smell of the hamburger in my hand spurred me on. I pressed the doorbell again, holding it down this time. I knew Victor was inside somewhere.

"Darlin', darlin', darlin', where's the fire?" The Southern belle made her appearance. She was short, barely coming up to my chin, and almost as round as she was tall. She was dressed in a flowing caftan and flip-flops. A mop of greasy graying hair hung limply about her face, and her lips were painted in a crookedly applied garish pink. She had an insulated mug in one hand and a cigarette in the other. "Come on in, welcome to our humble home," she said, gesturing widely into the dark interior.

No way was I stepping foot inside this bizarre scene. "I'm just here to drop this off. I don't want to take up too much of your time. If you would just let Victor know I'm here, I'll be on my way."

She stood silently for an eerie moment, her eyes narrowing as she regarded me. She took a deep breath and yelled loudly, staring straight in my eyes. "Victor, you dumb darkie, get down here right now. You got a pretty lady visitor here at the door."

My head snapped back in surprise, yet I met her glare with a steady gaze. "Thank you so much. I'll just wait here on the porch for him."

I turned from her and sat down on the dusty bench. She stood a moment longer and then heaved the door shut, slamming it loudly. I flinched. I really wanted to run away, but there was no way I was going to leave without Victor. I sat for a few minutes, taking a deep breath, sneaking a look at my phone to see how long I had been there. Ten minutes. It seemed like an eternity. I heard shuffling behind the closed door, then muffled, angry words. The door flew open and there stood darling Delores and Victor. He had on the same shirt he was wearing the last time I had seen him. It had food and who knows what all down the front. His face had the characteristic wrinkled forehead that by now I knew meant he was deeply distressed. His pants were wrinkled, and he looked as though he had not slept a wink since I had seen him two days ago.

"Hey, my friend!" I smiled, ignoring Delores. "I brought you the Victor special." I extended my hand with the McDonald's bag toward him. As he reached for it, Delores's hand shot out as quickly as a snake and grabbed it from me.

"What have we here? I love me a good frenchie fry. I'm sure our little darkie won't mind sharing with me, would you darlin'?"

She spoke to Victor but looked right at me, challenge in her eyes. Victor stood dumbly mute, looking back and forth between us, animosity hanging heavy in the air.

"Oh, yes ma'am," I said, laying it on thick, my best sarcastic Texas twang. "Don't we all just love a good fry, and after all, you do look hungry, so by all means, help yourself." I waited, one eyebrow raised.

She coughed loudly and shoved the bag toward Victor, spilling some fries at the feet of the old man in the corner who just grunted. She kicked the fries toward him. "Another dumb darkie. This one don't even talk, just takes up space. There you go, that's your lunch, dummy, just eat it. That's all you get until you find your tongue and talk like everyone else!" She then looked at me and gestured grandly toward the bench. "Why don't you have a sit out here? Looks like we need to have us some conversation. I'll be right back." She said it as if we were about to have an afternoon tea and disappeared inside the house. Victor, saying nothing, sat in a chair opposite but did not open his bag of food.

"Go ahead and eat. We won't be long. Then we'll throw the bike in the Jeep and go," I said in a low voice.

"Oh, he ain't goin' nowhere, honey." Delores reappeared suddenly, holding something close to her bosom that I could not see. "We got some business to take care of," she said, plopping down beside me.

On the low table in front of us was a large, dusty Bible with an ashtray on top. She set aside the ashtray and placed a slice of American cheese on top of the Bible. She reached into her caftan, pulled out a rat, and set it atop the Bible. The rat fell upon the cheese instantly, and she sat back with a triumphant look on her face, waiting for my reaction. "That's Jezebel, she's my pet, my best friend, really." She smiled widely.

"She's adorable," I said, smiling through my gritted teeth. There was no way I was going to give this woman the satisfaction of seeing me run screaming from this bizarre house of horrors.

She stretched forward and, picking up Jezebel and turning it on its side, pointed to a bulging mass on the rat's right side. "See this here? That's a tumor. The vet said there ain't nothin' he can do about it."

I swallowed, disgusted. "I'm so sorry to hear about that," I replied.

She held Jezebel out to me, and cackling, she said, "Here, you can pet her. She don't bite."

Sitting up very straight I looked at this woman in the eyes and, reaching out my hand, scratched the ugly rat between the ears. Thankfully, it lay on its side in her hand, quite still. "Poor thing," I said to the rat. At this point I even felt sorry for the animal that it had to live with this obviously disturbed woman.

Delores carefully set the rat on the bench between us, and it scurried behind her and up onto her shoulder. It sat there, cleaning its ears with its front paws, oblivious to my revulsion at the woman on the bench next to me. About this time the angry man came out the door and, without a word, sat on the ground at Delores's feet. He lit a cigarette and sat there saying nothing.

"So," said Delores, reaching out and caressing the young man's hair in front of her.

He slapped at her hand. "Don't touch me," he complained.

Delores continued as if nothing had happened. "We need to talk about this darkie here," she said, gesturing toward Victor, who was still sitting quietly clutching his McDonald's bag. "Eat your food, dummy, before it gets cold. This here lady was nice enough to bring it to you."

He flinched at the sound of her harsh voice. He rattled the

bag open and, hunching over, obediently began to eat. Turning her attention back to me, she asked, "So how'd you get hooked up with this one? His momma is a crack addict, and he's just a dumb know-nothin' off the street. No value whatsoever. Lazy as the day is long, just standin' around on street corners."

Victor's head snapped up from his burger. "She not a crack addict. I don't like it when you say that."

She hushed him loudly. "You don't know what you sayin'. She an addict. I should know. I'm a trained psychotherapist. I went to a very prestigious university, and I know all about these things. I could have had a real lucrative career, but I'm real dedicated to helpin' these guys here."

She turned to me once more, having now adopted a new accent. This time British. "In my years at university I learned all about addiction and mentally ill people. That's why I know I can help all these street people here," she said, gesturing to her little band of inmates on the porch with us. "Take Mike here, for example," pointing to the man sitting in front of her, "he's a prime specimen of a fine man that the government got all messed up on medication. They say he's bipolar, but I got him right off the street and off that medicine. What he needs is love, a lot of love." She caressed him and giggled. "And a good hot meal. If a man has a good woman, that's all he needs to get right in the head. Right honey, that's all you need," she crooned in Mike's ear.

He flinched and flicked his cigarette butt into the bushes with dozens of others. "I just need people to leave me alone," he spat angrily.

Delores straightened her frock primly and addressed me once more. "I learned all about these people in school. That's why I pick them up off the streets and give them a place to stay, so they can get back on their feet. I help them get their Social Security money too, so I can take care of them," she announced proudly.

I was developing a loud ringing in my ears the more she talked. She was crazy. A crazy lady picking up mentally ill men off the street, bringing them into her home, and collecting their Social Security. It was nothing short of illegal.

As thoughts raced through my mind, she began telling a story about a neighbor's garage burning down. "We don't know nothing about that, do we, lovies?" she simpered. About this time a young lady, likely no more than seventeen, came striding across the porch. Her skin was a beautiful light mocha, and dark curly ringlets bounced about her heart-shaped face. She was rail thin and model tall, with a backpack over her shoulder, four-inch heels, and a phone firmly stuck to her ear. She sauntered past all of us as if we were invisible, into the dark depths of the house.

"Violet," Delores called stridently after the disappearing form. Turning back to me, she said, "That's my daughter Violet. I'm real proud of her. Straight As in school. She's going to get a scholarship for sure."

I sat disbelieving, but said quickly, "That's wonderful. You must be so proud." Then, I asked, "She lives here with you?" I wondered how this beautiful young girl could live here in this house with all these obviously mentally ill men and her even more disturbed mother.

"Oh, yes I am. She's going to follow in my footsteps for sure. She'll be famous someday, you just mark my words!" She sat back with a satisfied sigh and looked out over the yard to the street beyond. She was still. I was edgy and ready to leave but sensed she had more to say, and I was oddly compelled to listen. Like watching a scary movie and yet not being able to look away.

She scratched the rat on her shoulder absently for a moment, her eyes wandering across the motley assortment of guests sitting on her front porch. Her expressions rolling across her face with each person her eyes beheld, like waves crashing on the seashore. Victor hunched over his hamburger, eyes darting about nervously; the toothless man in the corner, tracing a line in the dust with his finger and humming quietly; and the flat-eyed Mike at her feet, nonchalantly lighting up his third cigarette. Then her gaze fell on me. She asked in a low and deadly voice, thrusting her chin in Victor's direction, "What you want with him?"

"Want? I don't want anything *from* him. I want to help him."

She cackled loudly. "Help him? Girl, I have cleaned him up more times than I can remember. He'll just go right back to that same old corner and piss himself like he always does. He's lazy, that's his problem. Boy don't want to work, just wants to sleep all the time."

"Well, I understand that. However, I know that God wants me to help him, so that's what I'm going to do," I challenged.

"God? What you know about God? I know more about God in my little finger than you, missy." She picked up the Bible in front of her and wiped the dust and cheese from the cover. She waved it under my nose. "Everything I need to know is right here. I live and die by this book."

"Oh, that's wonderful," I replied, nodding. "Then of course you understand very well why it's important for me to follow the call of God in this matter. I'm quite sure that we are on the same page about Victor." I stood. I was finished with this lady, her scary house, and the flat-eyed man. Enough was enough. Who knew what was going on in this house? "I've taken up too much of your day. I'm heading out. Victor, why don't you go get your things?" I asked, looking over Delores's head in his direction.

He jumped up quickly, but she was quicker. "He's not goin'

anywhere with you. He's staying right here with me. Ain't you honey?" She rubbed his arm and stood close to his side. Victor looked at me with desperation in his eyes.

"I think he is quite capable of making his own decisions. He is a grown man, after all," I said to her.

"Uh, I g-g-g-guess I'm alright," he stuttered, stumbling over his words. "I'll call you if I need something else."

Delores cackled triumphantly, a wide smile across her face. My heart was breaking.

"That's fine then." I forced a smile. "Talk to you tonight, my friend. Delores, it was a pleasure meeting you." I held out my hand, but she ignored it.

"Come on, everybody, let's get in the house before miss goody two shoes tries to help you too. She thinks I don't know what I'm doing around here." She held the door wide and I saw the challenge in her eyes.

"No, ma'am," I answered quietly, so only she could hear. "I think you know exactly what you're doing, and I do too."

In that moment I knew I could not force Victor to want my help, or to choose me over someone who didn't have his best interests at heart. I turned on my heels and hurried to my car, tears brimming. I started the Jeep quickly and backed out of the driveway and headed away from the house of horrors as hot tears began to rain down my cheeks. It felt like I had a rock in my stomach. Nothing good was going to happen there. I drove a few miles and pulled over into an empty parking lot. I jammed the car into park and exhaled deeply, leaning my head back against the headrest.

"Lord," I prayed aloud. "I've got nothing for this. I can't do anything about that woman. She's scary. Victor's scared of her, and I am too. She's not stable. What in the world am I supposed to be doing? Did I hear You wrong? Was I not supposed to help him? Did I make it all up? I can quit. I can let him go. I can't make him want help. You have to do something about this."

I sat in silence, thinking about the otherworldly experience I just had. I exhaled, utterly drained. Coffee. After all that, I needed coffee. I drove a few blocks to the nearest Starbucks and headed inside, intending to sit among some regular people for a while and try to get the Stephen King movie reel out of my head. I joined a young mom with a cute little baby on her hip in line. The sight of such a sweet little face, some normalcy, and the aroma of the coffee calmed me. I stepped up and placed my order, "Tall latte, extra hot, no foam, three raw sugars." As I dug to the bottom of my purse for the wallet, my phone rang. Juggling my wallet, keys, and the phone, I saw it was Victor.

I smiled a thank-you to the cashier, handed her my credit card, and answered the phone all at one time. "Hello?"

"Hey!" Victor said, puffing and out of breath. "Where are you?" he asked loudly.

"I'm at Starbucks. Where are you?"

"I'm on the main road. Delores got real mad after you left. She started screaming at everyone and throwing things. When she wasn't looking, I got on my bike and left. I don't think she'll come after me, but can you come get me?"

Music to my ears. The barista was calling my name as I ran out the door, coffee forgotten. As I sped down the road I thanked God for the answered prayer. He is always amazing that way.

Down the middle of the street came Victor, pedaling for all he was worth, bent over the handlebars. Walmart grocery sack with his change of clothes hanging from the handlebars. I pulled into the nearest driveway and waited. He pulled up and jumped off his bike. I went to him and gave him a giant hug. He was breathing hard, sweaty, and smelled like fear, with his eyes still darting about.

I pulled the latch on the back of the Jeep. "Come on, throw that baby in here and let's roll."

"Yeah!" he said. I grabbed the handlebars in the front and he grabbed the back tire. We shoved the bike in, giving no thought to upholstery or scratches, just wanting to get as far away as fast as possible. We walked to our respective doors, jumped in, and drove away.

"What, Victor, in the world was *that* all about?" I asked.

He glanced over at me, wiping the sweat from his forehead with a napkin. "What?" he asked, puzzled.

"*What?*" I nearly screeched. I took a deep breath and said, calmly as possible, "The crazy lady with the rat and the Bible and the man with no teeth. What was that? She knows your mother? You stayed with her before? That was awful!"

"Aw, it's not so bad. She just gets mad sometimes," he said, trying to placate me, even going so far as to give me a reassuring pat on the arm.

I gaped. "Are you kidding me? You looked like you were terrified of the woman!"

He was patting my arm faster now. "Naw, naw, I'm fine. I don't go there to see her. I go there to see her daughter, Violet. She seems real sad sometimes, and I just try to be a good friend to her."

Ah. Now it made sense. I rolled my eyes. "Are you kidding me? You put up with all of that for a pretty girl?"

"Yeah, yeah, of course! Did you see her?" Victor answered with a huge smile.

By this time I was back at Starbucks, and I had to laugh at him. "Let's go inside. I have a cup of coffee with my name on it, and I'll even spring for a cocoa for you. I can't wait to hear all about your friend Delores."

After our coffee break, I deposited Victor back at the hotel. He rolled his bike inside, dropped his bag of clothes on the floor, fell face-first on the bed, and was almost instantly asleep. I called Dean and gave him the condensed version of the circus that was my afternoon. Later, I took stock of the room as Victor gently snored. He looked like a small child, innocent, and finally at peace. I began to pick up food wrappers and empty soda cans and realized the trash can was overflowing. Apparently, he had not let the cleaning lady in to take care of his room. I gathered all the trash, piled the wet towels in the bathtub, wiped the sticky desk and bathroom counters, and took a load of dirty clothes to the laundry room.

This is what Dean and I had wanted to know, the very reason we had taken him to a hotel, to see whether he was capable of taking care of himself. I looked around and realized he was not. He needed someone to check on him, to make sure he took his medicine, and to remind him to put on clean clothes and brush his teeth. And, after the incident with Delores, I now understood that he did not have the ability to discern a person's intent, good or bad.

Several volunteers and I had been calling all over the city trying to find a place for him. The truth was, though, even if we found a place, I was certain he would refuse to stay there. He craved stability with the same people taking care of him. This is where family comes in, and why he fell through the cracks. If there is no support system, how can someone living on the street ever overcome their circumstances?

I continued to clean the room, then folded the now dry clothes and put them away. I locked the door and closed it gently, satisfied that he would sleep all day and the fire department would check on him in the evening. Since Delores had his phone number, I also got him a new number that day. But as long as she knew where he was, he was not safe. It would be too easy for him to end up back on the street, and I did not want that to happen.

I dragged myself home that evening feeling utterly discouraged. The reality that this whole scenario rested squarely with Victor was finally sinking in. I could not force him to abide by my rules or for that matter even keep him off the street. Walking in the door I found a hot pizza and a husband eager to hear about my day. After a hug we sat down, and I helped myself to a large slice; I realized I had not eaten all day. I shared my day's adventure while he listened, mouth agape.

"No way, I do not believe she had a rat. You're making that up!" he said disbelievingly.

"I kid you not. It is the honest truth. That was the most bizarre experience of my whole life. These are the kind of people 'helping' Victor. The guy literally does not stand a chance," I said with resignation.

Dean chewed thoughtfully and, around a mouthful of pizza, said, "You know, don't you, that we can't keep him at that hotel? And that if we move him, it sounds like she'll just find him again."

I nodded. "My thoughts exactly. You have any ideas?"

"I think we need to bring him here." Just like that, he said it.

It was really what I had been thinking all along but felt it was too much to ask of my husband. Now, however, Dean was laying it out on the table, right over the cooling pizza. I sat back. "Are you sure about that? I mean, I think it's the right thing to do too. But I'm just thinking about our tiny house. I'll have to clear out my office. That's the only space for him. We'll have no privacy."

And as it says in Luke 14:28–33, we counted the cost:

> Suppose one of you want to build a tower. Won't you first sit down and estimate the cost to see if you have enough money to complete it? For if you lay the foundation and are not able to finish it, everyone who sees it will ridicule you, saying, "This person began to build and wasn't able to finish."
>
> . . . In the same way, those of you who do not give up everything you have cannot be my disciples.

We sat there that night and talked it through, knowing the Lord was asking us to do something huge: to turn our lives upside down for this sweet man who had nothing. It was momentous. In the end, we agreed that it was the right thing to do.

Dean stood, picking up his jacket from the back of his chair. "Well, no time like the present. Ready to go pick up our new roommate?"

I smiled. "Yes, I think so."

CHAPTER 13

Coming Home

We drove to the hotel to pick up Victor, who came with us happily, packing up his meager belongings and following us to the car as if he were on his way to grandma's house. We cleaned out my office so he could have his own space, leaving all my work stuff piled on the floor in our bedroom. I would figure out what to do with them later. We celebrated the occasion with ice cream, with Victor sitting up very tall at our small kitchen table, ice cream dripping over his hand and onto the floor; the dogs happily mopped up after him.

We explained to him that we didn't want him to be lonely at the hotel, which he accepted with no questions asked. In truth, though, knowing where he was at all times (being that it was too far for him to get to the corner alone) made things easier for me, as every day I visited the Social Security office or had meetings with someone who might be able to help.

Those first weeks were rather stiff and uncomfortable, although I could see how hard Victor was working to clean up after himself and be polite. He would spend the better part of every day napping on the couch, which left us, as we had anticipated, with very little privacy in the house. He was nervous when I left without him, even though I had reassured him we were fine and urged him to make himself at home.

At the cooking school it was time for kids cooking camp, requiring me to get up early, do my Bible study, and be out until late afternoon, leaving Victor alone for much of the day. I was elbow deep in camp each week that summer with sixteen wildly enthusiastic chefs, ages seven through twelve. I was running a business, keeping my home clean, feeding my family, and attending to Victor.

In the midst of all this, Victor's story was picked up by a local news station. A reporter called me right at the end of one of my kids camp classes, wanting to know if Victor and I would consent to telling our story on the local news. It was on a day I was shorthanded because my dishwasher had called in sick. I had flour and butter in my hair and was up to my elbows in a sink full of dirty dishes with many more in bus tubs on the floor. To say I was tired and distracted would be an understatement. So when I answered the phone, it was one of those out-of-left-field moments.

"Well, I would be happy to ask Victor if that is something he would like to do. Today? In two hours?" I eyed the mountain of dirty dishes warily; they seemed to somehow be multiplying. As I glanced down at the floor to take a deep breath and gather my thoughts, I noticed chocolate and something sticky-looking on the top of my shoe. *Ah, what the heck,* I thought. *Victor will love it. He's the most eloquent person I know, a total natural for an interview, and he has such positive thoughts to share.* So, with a deep breath and straightened back, I said, "You bet. I can make two hours happen."

The next hour was a blur. I called Victor and urged him to shower and dress, called Dean to let him know there would be a news crew in the living room when he got home, and blew through those dishes like a Category 5 hurricane. I turned off the lights, locked the door, then put the pedal to the metal on the way home. Then the realization hit me that I had left early that morning with the bed unmade, dirty dishes in the sink, and a slightly smelly dog sleeping upside down on the couch.

When I got home, Victor was sitting at the kitchen table eating a bowl of cereal with his usual sweet, slightly sleepy look on his face. "Are you ready?" I ran in asking. "Have you showered? You have a spot on your shirt!" I spoke while tossing dirty dishes in the oven because the dishwasher was full, and hiding unfolded clean clothes in the hall closet. "Can you put the dog outside and fluff the couch pillows? What about your bed? Did you make it today? Never mind, just close your door. What about your fingernails? Do they need to be clipped? Oh, my goodness, I need to take a shower. Okay, no time for that. They can't smell us on TV anyways, right?"

I finally turned around, hands dripping soapy water onto the kitchen floor. Victor was standing in the middle of the kitchen holding his cereal bowl, looking somewhat afraid to approach the sink. He stared at me like I was an alien. "Are you gonna be alright?" His concern was written all over his face.

I realized at that moment that I had appeared to have lost my mind. This man loves peace, quiet, and calm. Time to refocus. I held out my soapy hand for his cereal bowl. "Yes, I'm all right. A little wound up maybe, but all right."

"Oh good. You need to stay calm now, okay?"

By this time, I was tired and feeling lightheaded from all my dashing around. A nap seemed like a good idea. But instead, as comrades in arms together, we hid all the mess, closed all the doors, lit a candle, and greeted the newscaster a full eighteen minutes later. I even had time to put on a little lipstick and use a bit of butter to slick my hair into a messy bun on top of my head.

It's no exaggeration to say that after the news story aired that night, chaos descended upon our house. I was sitting peacefully at the kitchen table the next morning with my Bible and Dean sipping his coffee quietly opposite me, when his phone beeped. He looked at it, set it carefully on the table, and said, "Did you know that the story from the news last night went viral? You and Victor are on the front page of Yahoo this morning."

I gaped. "What? No way!" I picked up my phone, which had been on silent. It was blowing up as I watched, and continued ringing as the day progressed. I left the messages unanswered and went to work. Thankfully, the kids were unimpressed by anything not having to do with homemade pizza.

After class I again picked up my phone and was stunned by all the calls, emails, and text and Facebook messages. Utterly overwhelmed, I put it aside and returned to the dishes. As I scrubbed I prayed, *Lord, what in the world am I supposed to do with all this?* It was never my intent to draw attention to myself. I just wanted some ideas on what could be done to help Victor.

Matthew 6:1 quickly sprang to mind: "Be careful not to practice your righteousness in front of others to be seen by them. If you do, you will have no reward from your Father in heaven." As I rinsed the dishes, a sense of peace flooded my soul. The Lord knew my intent. And this was an opportunity to share the goodness of God. I knew this was a chance to "let the one who boasts boast in the Lord" (2 Cor. 10:17). After finishing with the dishes, I sat down to answer the messages, feeling thrilled at the opportunity to share our story and talk about how God had redeemed Victor from the street, just as He had redeemed me from my sin.

There followed over the next weeks a dizzying array of interviews with media from all over the world. We were on CNN and even a radio program in India. During this time, I have come to learn about the control the media has over content. I would talk about Jesus during the interviews, and they would cut it out every time, except for something Victor said in one interview that was shared in several media outlets:

"She helped me. It's like grace," he said.

His innocent words, and the knowledge that the interviewer, the cameraman, and crew had heard about His goodness was enough for me. I knew that God would make His name known in His time.

CHAPTER 14

Mother Hubbard

One day I received a Facebook message from a man who said he was Victor's cousin from West Texas. He said he was astounded and heartbroken that his cousin had been having such a hard time and asked me to please call him. Giving it little thought, I picked up the phone and gave him a call.

"Hi, this is Ginger. You sent me a message on Facebook about Victor?"

The response was immediate, and loud. "Oh, thank *gawd*, I'm so glad you called me! I had no idea Vic was living on the street. You gotta believe me, ma'am. I was making deliveries on that side of town a few months ago. I probably even drove by him. I just feel awful!" said a deep voice on the other end of the line.

"Oh? Really? How are you related to Victor?" I asked, not sure how to handle this. I was wary of talking to people I did not know, especially when contacted online.

"Yes, ma'am, Vic is my cousin. We grew up together. I sure had no idea he was living like that. I saw that Facebook page and

I just cried and cried. You gotta believe me, I had no idea he was living like that."

This guy sure sounded sincere. I was softening a bit. "What's your name?"

"It's Dwayne, ma'am. I'm Vic's cousin. My dad is his mother Corvina's brother."

"Oh, I see. Have you seen your aunt Corvina in the last few years?"

"Oh, no ma'am, last I saw her, we was all living in West Texas, then she moved off to Houston to be with Vic's sister. She brought Vic to my house to stay after she moved."

"And how long ago was this?" I asked, perplexed at the details of the story so far.

"Around about ten years or so now. I got down on my luck and moved to Houston to find better work."

"And so, when you moved, what happened to Victor if he was living with you?"

"Oh, we went to your town there and dropped him off at his sister's house. That's where his mom was staying. That's the last I saw of him, till I saw him today on Facebook. It says he was living on the streets, is that true?"

"Yes, it's true. He's been on and off the streets that entire time. You never looked him up all these years? Or had a family get-together?" I was perplexed with this whole thing.

"Naw, our family is not real close, so I never thought to look him up. I wondered from time to time, but I knew Vic always took care of hisself."

Nonplussed, I said in a low voice, "I don't know about that. When I befriended him he was in really bad shape."

"My daddy is going to be so upset, you have no idea, Miss Ginger. We really love each other, and this will just do him in."

I began tapping my pencil on the desk. “Seems like if you love each other so much, you would check in from time to time, wouldn’t you?” My suspicious side was flaring up again. I didn’t know whether to trust this guy or not.

“We . . . we just lost touch is all. Where do you live? Can I come see Vic?”

“What? Oh, I don’t know about that.” I sure as heck was not giving this guy my address.

“Can I talk to him?”

“Um, actually no, you can’t talk to him. I don’t know if that would be a good idea. I have a question for you. Was Victor normal when he was a kid? Did he have any kind of health issues or was he slow?”

“Slow? I don’t know. He was always real thoughtful and quiet, but he was okay. Why?”

“Well, he has some issues that make me think perhaps he has some kind of family health history, and it concerns me,” I said.

“Well, I will tell you this, when he was nineteen he got sick somehow. He was in the hospital for a while. That was right before his momma took off to Houston and he came to stay with me and the other cousins.”

“So, what was that like, when he came to stay with you?” I was happy that I was actually getting some information from someone who knew Victor, even if I didn’t trust him farther than I could throw him.

“He slept a lot, never wanted to shower or go to the club. He drank some, but mostly he slept. Not like the old Vic for sure,” he said in a lower tone. “It made me sad.”

“I bet it did. I know he’s a kind and gentle person. I can only imagine what he must have been like before,” I agreed.

We spoke for a few more minutes, and he expressed that

he would love to come see Victor sometime. I said perhaps we could meet halfway. Although he had for the most part seemed a pleasant person, I didn't want to give away too much personal information. As we hung up the phone, I reflected on the story he offered up. *Talk about layers of the onion*, I thought. I had no idea then, but we were just getting started.

Late that evening the phone rang, and I almost did not answer. There had been nonstop interviews with the media, and I was tired.

"Miss Ginger, this here is LaMont. Victor's uncle. I'm here in Clear Lake. I just drove in from West Texas. I looked up your business on the internet, and I'm here in front of Art of the Meal."

"Excuse me?" I questioned sharply. "Who is this again?"

"I'm Dwayne's daddy. He talked to you this afternoon. I jumped right in the car and came to Clear Lake to see Victor. Where do you live? I'll come to your house."

By this time I had put the phone on speaker so Dean could hear the conversation. He quickly motioned, shaking his head no. "No, I don't think so, LaMont. It's already 9:00 p.m. Maybe we can meet for breakfast in the morning?" No way was I going to let someone roll into town and see Victor without knowing who he was. Momma Bear came out in full force that night.

"Oh, Miss Ginger, I just drove in and I don't even have a place to stay. I just need to put my eyes on Victor and make sure he's okay. We seen him on the news."

"Well, if you saw him on the news then you know he's just fine." It did not escape me that the newscaster also spoke at length about the generosity of the community in giving to the GoFundMe for Victor's care, which was by this time at a staggering twenty thousand dollars. Call me suspicious, but here comes the family all of a sudden from out of the woodwork, terribly worried about Victor?

"Well, Miss Ginger, can I at least talk to Vic?" he asked.

Dean nodded, and leaving the phone with him, I walked into Victor's room. He was watching MTV as usual. "Hey Victor, do you have an Uncle LaMont?"

"Yeah, why?" he asked.

"Well, he's on the phone in the other room. He saw you on TV and wanted to talk to you."

"Yeah? Cool, I'll talk to him."

I could not tell by his expression whether or not he was excited by the prospect. But as he picked up the phone and began to talk, his voice became animated, and his natural family vernacular began to show in his speech. Dean and I grinned at each other. It was good to see him smile. After a few minutes he covered the phone and asked, "Uncle LaMont is at Taco Bell. You think we could go meet him?" His eyes were bright and excited.

I sighed. "Of course, Victor, let me get my shoes. Tell him twenty minutes." He was ecstatic and told his uncle we would meet him.

"Is this a good idea?" Dean asked under his breath as he grabbed the car keys.

"Who knows. But I would like to find out more about his past. Maybe the uncle knows where his mom is, and we can unravel this whole family drama. Maybe there's someone in his family who would like for him to come back home."

"Good point," Dean answered. "Let's go find out."

Victor's uncle drove a brand-new Chevy pickup, sparkling white, four-door extended cab. He leaped out of the truck as we drove up, and he and Victor hugged happily. He seemed like a nice man, well-spoken and polite, taking many pictures of Victor and himself with his iPhone. We chatted for a while there in the parking lot, then Dean and I asked LaMont if he would like to go inside and sit and visit a bit. But he said, "No, ma'am, I've got to get back on the road and get home. I just wanted to make sure Victor was all right with my own eyes. You two look like you're doing a real good job taking care of him." He slapped Dean heartily on the back. "Keep up the good work!" He then turned and jumped quickly into his truck. I was flabbergasted. I could not believe he was just going to leave. No offer to help? No offer to take Victor back home to this large extended family I kept hearing about? Something was off here.

"Wait!" I said loudly. "Do you at least know where his mother is?" I asked desperately.

"His momma?"

"Yes, LaMont, your sister. Do you know where she might be?" I was getting irritable.

"Oh, I don't know. I haven't talked to her in about five years. Saw her here in Clear Lake, and Victor too. They seemed to be doing just fine," he said nonchalantly.

"Well, we really need to get in touch with her. Do you have any ideas where she might be?"

"Hey," Victor interjected. "My sister lives close to here. She won't talk to me much. Maybe she'll tell you where my momma is?"

"Oh, well, I guess I could do that. What's the address?"

Uncle LaMont wasted no time and offered to go see her. I did not point out that it was going on 11:00 p.m. and perhaps a little late to be knocking on someone's door. But if his trip might find Victor's mother, who was I to tell him what to do? We agreed he would go knock on her door while the three of us we went back home, then reconvene for breakfast in the morning.

Victor slept late the next day. I kept waiting to hear from LaMont but didn't hear from him all morning. Finally, around noon, my phone rang.

"Hey, Miss Ginger, this here is LaMont. I'm here with Victor's mother. She wants to talk to him." I could hear talking and clanking in the background. I was utterly stunned.

"His mother? You found her? Just like that?"

"Yes ma'am, his sister had her address. I came right over here last night. She just fine. Just real upset because she hasn't been able to find Victor for the last six months. Here she is." I heard a brief muffled conversation, then a strident voice came over the phone.

"Who is this? What you doing with my son? You need to bring him to me right now. You got no business with him." Not what I expected.

"How do you do, ma'am? You've been looking for Victor for six months? He was at the same corner where you saw him last. Not for six months, but for about three years."

"You do not get sassy with me, Miss Ginger. You just bring my son to me, and I don't need no judgment from you. I don't like your tone."

My hackles raised, I responded, "Nor I yours, ma'am. I will not bring Victor to you until you and I sit down and have a conversation about him."

"I ain't having no conversation with you! You bring me my son, or I will come get him. Let me talk to him." She was getting loud. Really loud.

"No ma'am, again, I will not."

Click. She hung up.

I raised my eyebrows. *I am not calling this lady back.* Two minutes later she called back, same conversation, same click at the end. Victor was in the other room, so I stepped outside. The third time she called, I spoke respectfully, "If you would like the opportunity to see Victor, I will meet you and we can discuss it. Where would you like to meet?"

"Well, I need you to come here where I am. I ain't got no car," she relented.

"That's fine," I responded. "I'm happy to meet you where it's convenient." Thirty seconds later I had an address and a plan to meet his mother in less than an hour. I looked up her address and immediately felt sick. It was a mere ten minutes from where poor Victor had stood on the corner for so long.

I positioned myself in a booth at the McDonalds's near her house where we had agreed to meet; dead center in a big picture window so I could see the street. The plastic booth was cold and so was I. Confrontation is not my thing, and I had no idea if this woman would be stark-raving mad or crafty as a snake. In any other circumstance I would have rehearsed a hundred times what I was going to say to someone, but this time I was drawing a complete blank. I felt like I was watching a movie unfold in slow motion.

I gazed out the window, waiting. It was a bright, beautiful day, and I knew the sun would be in her eyes as she walked toward the restaurant. Nervously sipping my now cold coffee, I saw her coming from a long way off and watched her every step. My stomach was in knots, and my anxiety was making me feel nauseous. As she approached the door, I could begin to make out her features. She was petite and very trim; nicely dressed in dark slacks and a pretty pink sweater with shiny black loafers. Her silver-streaked hair was swept up behind her head in a dignified bun that was as neat and tidy as she was. Her face was devoid of makeup except for some expertly applied gloss that finished off the look of a well-put-together lady. As she placed her hand on the door, I straightened automatically. Stepping inside, she squinted slightly as her eyes adjusted to the indoor lighting. I sat still. There would be no hand raised in greeting or hello from across the room from me. I simply sat there as she scanned the room. Then her eyes met mine. She stood for a moment longer, then gave a slight nod, straightened her shoulders, and walked slowly toward the booth.

As she neared, I stood and said, "Ms. Corina?"

"Yes. Where is my son?" she asked me loudly, the angry edge in her voice not matching her dignified demeanor.

"He's at my house. I told you I wanted to speak with you before I brought Victor to see you."

"So, you know where he is?"

I felt slightly irritated. "Yes, ma'am, that's what I said."

"Oh, thank *gawd*. I had no idea where he was!" She burst into noisy tears. I stood there unsure of what to do, except to give her a few awkward pats on the shoulder.

"He's fine, Ms. Corina. Can I get you a cup of coffee?"

"No, no, I just need my son!" She was loud, and people were staring.

"Why don't we have a seat and talk for a bit?" I asked.

"I just want to see my son!" The tears were gone, replaced by an angry, defiant squint in her watery eyes.

"Well, that's not going to happen right at this moment. And I want to talk to you and then decide whether or not it's best that you see Victor." With that, I sat down in the booth with an equally defiant squint in my eyes. She hesitated a few beats, then slid in also.

"Are you sure I can't get you anything?" I tried again.

"No, I'm fine. I just want my son."

I took a deep breath, the air between us was almost tangibly cracking. I had a feeling we were two strong-willed women, and neither of us, it seemed, was going to give an inch.

"I just want to know what you're doing with my son," she said again. Apparently, this was going to be the main theme of the conversation on her part.

"I'm not doing anything with him, ma'am. I've been helping him. Are you aware he has been on the street for the last several years?"

"He likes to be on the street. That's his choice," she replied.

"What?" I shook my head in disbelief. "No. He wasn't there because he liked it. He was there because he had nowhere else to go, and he was waiting for you. He was sleeping on the ground behind a restaurant."

"I know Vic. He always liked to stand on the corner. It gave him something to do during the day." She said it calmly, matter-of-factly, staring at me right in the eyes as if her steely gaze and determined delivery was going to somehow convince me his being on the street was a good thing.

"Regardless, Ms. Corina, of why he was there, he is staying with my family now until he gets on his feet."

"No, he ain't staying with you. Why you not listen to me? What I'm saying is that you're going to bring my son to me and leave him alone. He don't need no help from you."

I folded my arms and leaned back against the cold, plastic bench. I just looked at her, one eyebrow raised, and did not speak a word.

She stared at me for a few moments and then her forehead crinkled, and a few well-placed tears began to trickle down her cheeks. She dabbed delicately at the corners of her eyes. She said heavily, in a convincingly solemn tone, "Poor Vic. He was always different from the other kids. He was a special child, if you know what I mean."

"Yes, ma'am, I know exactly what you mean," I responded.

"Don't you go interrupting me now, you hear. I'm trying to tell you something." Annoyance filled her voice. "He was a hard child, but sweet. Never met a stranger. Always roaming around, but smart, real smart."

I nodded, but wisely kept silent.

"It's just real hard to manage him," she continued. "It helped when we had his Social Security money. We had some real good times then. I quit my job and we just stayed home together. Yes, those was real good times."

The anger rose up in a hard lump in my throat, but I did not speak. I knew now what I had suspected. His mother had been collecting his Social Security checks while Victor was sleeping on the corner for many months. I had discovered that the Social Security had only been discontinued six months before, but Victor was on the street long before that.

"So you going to take me to him now?"

Fear, apparently, had become my new friend. I was scared of Victor's mother; scared Victor would want to go with her, which clearly was a bad idea; and scared that he would end up right back on the street where I found him. I did not like Corina, and yet she had brought Victor into the world, a remnant of hope in the midst of chaos. Yes, she had abandoned him, but she, too, had a purpose.

My personal feelings aside, Victor loved her, even though

she had left him. It was not something he could verbalize, but I knew the bond between him and his mother was strong, overlooking the horror it had caused him. I respected that, even if I did not agree. Meeting Corina was the first in a long line of events that would lead me, in sheer gut-wrenching fear, to trust in the Lord to take care of the circumstances.

I liken it in some ways to my divorce. It was so very painful for me to see the kids go to Ben's house. I was abundantly aware that he didn't have the kindest things to say about me, and I worried that his words would lessen their love for me, that they would think worse of me than they already did, if that were even possible. I knew from experience the mere mention of my name would elicit a heavy sigh from Ben, an eye roll, and tense body language. The kids, so attuned they were to our feelings, knew his feelings toward me. Did I blame him? No. In the same way, I understood Corina wanted nothing to do with me because I was a reminder of her failure as a mother. Don't we all do that? Despise those who cause us to look back and see our error?

So many times it seems as though our errors would absolutely engulf us like a crashing ocean wave. Although we see it coming, we lack the energy to paddle fast enough to escape its force. So we just close our eyes and duck, throwing our hands over our heads. We feel it lift our feet as we are swept up and over, tumbling and gasping for breath. Disoriented, we shake the water from our eyes and, on days we are strong enough, quickly turn and swim to shore. But there are other days when we barely have time to recover before the next wave comes to beat us down again with its relentless strength.

I tried to remember that as I escorted Corina to my car that afternoon as we drove to the cooking school where Dean would be bringing Victor for the happy reunion. My familiar friend, fear, gripped my throat. "Do you need anything from the store? Could I buy you some groceries?" I asked. Victor's love for his mother compelled me to try to be kind to her. I figured if the Lord wanted me to love my enemies, I might as well roll with it, because I felt fairly confident that I had one sitting there right beside me in the car.

"Well, I could use one of those prepaid phone cards. Mine ran out," she said with a sideways glance.

"Of course, we can stop on the way," I said.

We rode in silence, quietly walking into a store to get what she needed, then headed back to the school. I was nervous as we sat inside waiting. Dean did not tell Victor that his mom would be there, being sure that he would be overjoyed. As their car pulled in, she stood beside a chair opposite the front door. Victor walked in the door ahead of Dean, then stopped short and stared for a moment.

"Momma, where you been?" He strode toward her in a quick, menacing manner that shocked me. "Where you been? I been waiting and waiting!" His voice quavered like a child's.

"Well now, Vic, I fell on some hard times. I told you I would come back to get you, so here I am. It's alright now. Don't you be causing a scene in front of these people," she said firmly and quietly.

"No, Momma, it's not alright. Where you been? These nice people had to help me. I got lots of friends now and I just wanted to make sure you were okay. I see you fine after all." Disappointment hung heavy in the air.

There was a bit more stilted small talk, as I could see that his mother really wanted to be alone with him. But I kept myself firmly planted on my barstool, as did Dean on the other side. We were going nowhere. After a while the conversation ground to a painful halt, and I said, "Well, Ms. Corina, I'm sure you're about ready to go back home now. How about Victor and I give you a ride back to your apartment?" She nodded slightly, and we proceeded quietly to the car.

Dean patted me reassuringly. "See you at the house."

The car ride was uncomfortably silent. We arrived at the apartment, and Victor and I walked her to the door.

"Vic, I think you need to stay here with me," she announced.

Victor began to answer but I cut him off immediately. "No ma'am, he will not. He does not have any of his things. Maybe another time." I could see she was very angry and wanted to argue, but I could see also that it was not going to happen in front of Victor. I pointed him toward the Jeep. "Time to go, Victor. We need to get home and make dinner." Then turning to Corina, "Good to see you, Ms. Corina."

She stood outside the door, hand on the knob, angry energy radiating from her like a nuclear reactor about to blow. We had not seen the last of her, I was sure.

In the car Victor was strangely silent. He sat with his knee thumping up and down and his hand tapping on the windowsill. As we pulled into the driveway he opened the door before the car had fully stopped. He went straight inside and closed the door of his room.

Dean lifted an eyebrow from the couch. "Good visit?"

"What do you think?" I said, pushing the dog aside and plopping down next to him. "I think she's going to be a problem."

"Ditto," he said in a low voice. I lay my head on his shoulder, my brain too tired to even dream up the next possible scenario to come.

The phone calls from Corina began the next day. Victor's phone rang at all hours of the day and night for days on end. She would tell him that a son's place was with his mother, and that he needed to come back and live with her immediately. I could see the tension on his face during those conversations and hear the strain in his voice as he strove to be patient with her.

Knowing how I felt about his mother, Victor reminded me that the Bible says to "honor your father and mother" (Ex. 20:12 NLT), and that he wanted to be faithful to the Lord. The phone kept ringing and, wanting to talk to her, he kept calling her too. Unfortunately, it was clear it wasn't going to end well.

To call the relationship dysfunctional would be an understatement. Wanting so desperately to talk to her and have a good relationship, he would call her immediately every time something good happened, hoping to please her. The day we received the news that his Social Security benefits had been granted, he called his mother to tell her the good news. I somehow could never get it through his mind that it was better not to tell her these types of things, particularly things pertaining to money, which was always a hot-button issue for her. I knew he called her because I could hear his raised voice booming behind his closed bedroom door. "What do you mean? She's not stealing my money, she's helping me!" Victor exclaimed loudly.

When he talked to his mother he always reverted to a teenager, complete with using "what" in every other sentence, which Momma did not care for at all. With a sigh, I slammed my near empty coffee cup down on the table. I tried to be nice, I tried to respect that he wanted to talk to his mother, I tried to see her side of the story, and I tried to remember her upbringing had been so very different from mine. But, that morning, with only one cup down, I'd had enough. Without even wiping up the spilled coffee,

I marched as angrily as my bare feet would allow across the tile floor and knocked loudly on his door. Loudly enough that Aaron poked his head out of his room immediately, only to duck back inside and lock his door when he saw my expression. Oh yeah, Mom was that mad.

I knocked loudly again on Victor's door, finally being heard over all the shouting that was going on. Outside the door I could hear his mother shouting, then all of a sudden, dead silence. *Ah,* I thought, *typical. She hung up.* I knew I had a two-minute reprieve.

"Come in," Victor said quietly. Hearing his weariness, my anger evaporated.

"Kind of early for fussing and fighting. What's wrong? Your momma mad?" I draped my arm over his slumped shoulder and gave him a squeeze.

He leaned against me briefly, straightening as the phone rang again. Raising it to his ear, he answered loudly. "What?"

Her ranting picked up right where she had left off. As the angry voices swirled around me, I sat at Victor's desk and tried to tune them out. I had heard it all before. As usual, it was enough to give a frustrated flavor to the entire day. By the end of the conversation, Victor would be exhausted and sleep the rest of the day; I would be annoyed; and his mother would be in a cab in front of our house, calling and threatening me to send her son outside to come home with her. Enough was enough.

I held out my hand. "Can I talk to her for a minute?"

"Yeah," he said, extending the phone.

"Hello Ms. Corina, how are you today?" I asked politely, interrupting her tirade.

"I'm fine," she said, stridently angry. "Let me talk to my son."

"No, ma'am, you are finished talking to Victor today. Is there something I can help you with?" I asked respectfully. I had no intention of being rude to her. As much as I disliked her, she was his mom, and by God, I was going to be nice even if it killed me.

"What you doing with my son? What you doing with that money? That money is mine. You stealing from him and I'm not going to put up with it!"

"Well, Ms. Corina, I'm not stealing from your son. That money is actually his, not yours. It's used for his benefit and will remain so. That's really not something that I'm going to discuss with you. Is there anything else you need today?" A click on the line signaled that she was gone again. I sighed. "Well, my friend, how about your phone takes a break in the other room and you take a quiet time?"

"Yeah, that's a good idea," he said, looking sad.

"Cheer up, maybe someday she won't be so cranky."

"Yeah, maybe. She said I got a lot of money. Is that true?"

"Well, I don't know about a lot of money. You got some to help with expenses, food, clothes, doctors, medicine."

"Oh, okay, well, I was wondering," he said. Then raising his eyes to meet mine, asked hopefully, "Do you think I should use that money to buy some gold teeth?"

"What?" I shook my head, utterly confused.

"You know, gold teeth, a grill, like the rappers on MTV."

"Gold teeth? *No*. No gold teeth. If you want gold teeth, that's something you're going to have to work and save up your money for. I'm pretty sure there are many more important things to save up your money for, like maybe an apartment?"

"Oh, okay, I just thought it would be a good idea. You don't think it's a good idea?" His brow was furrowed quizzically, disappointment written all over his face.

I sighed. "No, I really don't, Victor."

Late one afternoon the following week, Victor emerged from his bedroom, padding into the kitchen in his sock-clad feet, while I was washing dishes. He had been moody and remote since the last blowup with his mother.

"Finally decided to get out of bed, huh, Sleeping Beauty?" I teased. "Can I make you a sandwich?" He nodded and sat heavily at the kitchen table as I began pulling ingredients from the refrigerator.

"I want to go stay with my mom for a while," he said quietly. My heart sank. I lay the knife on the cutting board and sat opposite him at the table.

"We can go take her to lunch, so you can visit," I offered.

"No, I need to go stay with her for a while, then she'll leave me alone. She just worried about me, and I think she lonely." He never held a grudge. I could learn from this guy.

I sat for a moment, then resigned myself to his decision. "When do you want to go?"

"Tonight," he answered. "After my sandwich?" Talk about out of left field.

I rose so he could not see the hot tears spring up in my eyes. Clearing my throat, I said, "Can do. You go pack and I'll finish your sandwich, then I'll drop you off." I could not keep him; he had to want to be here. Some battles are only for the Lord to fight.

There was a heavy silence between us in the car that evening. Corina was pacing in the parking lot of her apartment building. She was on her phone as we drove up.

"You sure you don't want to just visit?" I asked Victor quietly. "She does not look very happy."

He shook his head silently.

I rolled the window down halfway as he climbed out of the Jeep and opened the back door to grab his duffel bag.

"How you today, Miss Ginger?" she sneered as she rushed up to the car.

"I'm fine, Ms. Corina. How are you?" I asked deadpan, not in the mood to play her game.

"Oh, I'm just fine. You don't have to worry about me."

"Wonderful, that's good to hear. No problems here either," I responded.

"Mmm hmm," she hummed. "I want to show you, I got me a new phone." She shoved an iPhone under my nose.

I raised my eyebrows. "That's good for you, Ms. Corina."

"Mmm humm, it is good for me. I will call my son when I feel like it. Oh yes, I will."

I nodded and forced a smile. I had to bite my tongue not to engage in any more conversation than was absolutely necessary. I watched in the rearview mirror as she walked to the back of my car and took a photo of the license plate. I sighed and pushed open the door with my foot and called out, "Would you care for my driver's license number too, Ms. Corina?"

"Oh no, ma'am, I got all I need right here." She smiled triumphantly, holding her new phone aloft.

"Oh good," I responded. "Glad to hear it. Just let me know if you need any additional information."

"Oh, I'll do that, don't you worry yourself about that."

She walked away proudly, with her head high, toward Victor, who was standing there on the sidewalk with a blank look on his face, hands hanging limply at his sides, and duffel bag at his feet. He looked exactly as he did the morning Dean and I left him on the corner in the rain. Abandoned. I sank down in my seat and tried to remind myself that it was his decision to stay with his mother, but this did not stop my heart from pounding in my chest or the clamminess of my palms.

I breathed out a prayer. "God, I know You are bigger than this situation. I know You are stronger. I know that I can cast my cares upon You. I'm casting, God. This is a hard one." I wanted to argue and fight and yell and tell her what an awful person she was. But in His grace, in my spirit, the Lord reminded me He died for her too.

"Come on, Vic, I got steak and some greens. I going to make you a nice dinner. I'm sure she don't know nothing about cooking like your momma," she said loudly, taking him by the arm.

She led him away that night. He was dragging his feet, looking back over his shoulder but saying nothing, looking for all the world like a prisoner headed to his last supper.

~

I called later that night to check on him, to remind him to take his medicine, and to make sure he was okay. It went straight to voice mail. I cried then, really cried, the ugly kind. Dean patted my back and reminded me that we were doing the right thing. We were trusting God. But it was hard. I resisted the urge to go knock on the door and make sure he was okay. It was an awful week. Dean and I thought perhaps we could enjoy a few days of having the house to ourselves again, but we could not. Even the dog lay in front of Victor's bedroom door forlornly, acting like he had lost his best friend.

I was at work, in the middle of getting ready for a big class, when Victor called. "Can you come get me?" I heard a raised voice I knew very well, loudly in the background.

"Absolutely. When will you be ready?" I asked, knowing I had several hours of work in front of me.

"Can you come now? I'm in the parking lot. My momma is mad." That was all I needed to hear.

"I'll be there in ten minutes." I dropped my knife, washed my hands, and locked the door behind me.

As I pulled into the apartment complex, Victor was waiting by the parking lot entrance. I slowed down, and he grabbed the door handle and leaped in, clutching his bag to his chest. "Hurry up, before she sees me!" he said as he slid down in his seat, breathing heavily. Surprised, I drove forward quickly, leaving the lot. "Here she comes, don't stop!" Sure enough, here came Momma Corina, running across the parking lot toward my car. "Don't stop, don't stop, don't stop," he chanted. I continued on across the lot as she picked up a rock and lobbed it in the direction of my car. I slanted a sideways glance toward my passenger, feeling better, despite the fact that I had an angry lady chasing me.

"Good visit?" I asked nonchalantly, eyebrow raised.

"Yeah, it was fine."

As we sat at the stop sign, I took in his dirty shirt stained with who knows what, then sniffed the air and smelled his body odor. "Yeah, I can see that. How about lunch?"

Over a burger he told me about his adventures of the past week. The first night was fine, he related. The steak was good, like he remembered. They talked about old times and family. But after that he said she would wake him at 3:00 a.m. to talk endlessly, and then become increasingly angry at his responses. He, in turn, would wander outside and roam the streets until she was not angry anymore.

Apparently, the night before he had ridden a borrowed bicycle some ten miles to James's house, an older man who was a "friend from the corner," which sounded a bit bizarre. Regardless, I could see the pattern with him: arguments with Mom, visiting friends, getting into trouble. It also became evident that this was how he had ended up on the street to begin with.

I thought we were good now. He had seen her and remembered how it was to live with her, and so would not be going back to her. Unfortunately, his remembrance would last only about a month, and then we would repeat the cycle. No amount of reminding on my part would change his mind when he felt he needed to go see her. It was a painful cycle we would walk out again and again over the next year.

CHAPTER 15

The Past Makes an Appearance

It was a Sunday, and Victor was back at his mom's house, or so I thought. It was almost laughable that on my day of rest, as I was walking in the door from church, there was Victor standing just inside the front door, bouncing on his heels and waving his hands about.

"My friend James called and invited me over. Can you take me to his house?"

"Who?" I queried, my mind too confused to even make the connection.

"My friend James. Remember I told you I went and saw him the other night when I was at my momma's house."

"Oh," I responded. I did remember.

He had told a bizarre story of a friend from the corner. A really nice friend, with a Mercedes, who would pick him up and take him to the "clubs" downtown. I didn't ask him what a person like that might want with a street person who smelled like a dumpster in the summer. The only thing I knew was that it would not be something good. Although Victor maintained it was all sweet innocence, I knew better. But I was also unwilling to argue.

Not wanting to encourage this so-called friendship, I knew it was time for tough love. "Well, you can go see your friend. I'll drop you off with your bike, but you'll have to ride home," I said, hoping this would discourage him, being that it was about an hour's bike ride from the house.

"Oh, that's okay, that's okay," he reassured me.

"Does he know you're coming over?" I asked.

"Oh, he doesn't have to know. He won't mind if I just show up," he said quickly.

"Uh, okay fine. Well, it's on you." Then, since we were going to see Dean's parents that day, I hoped to tempt him with one of his favorite foods. "Sorry you're going to miss barbecue."

"Oh, will you bring me some home?" he wheedled expectantly.

"Nope, sorry my friend, you want barbecue, you can go with us. I'm not bringing you take-out," I replied, sounding for all the world like the mom that I am.

"Oh, oh well. I'll probably eat at my friend's house anyways," he said thoughtfully.

"Yeah," I thought out loud, sadly, "I'm sure you will."

Dean said we were leaving in an hour, and despite my exhaustion, I began to clean the house like a mad woman. Sitting still was just not possible with my mind wondering how I could get Victor to change his mind about visiting his friend. As I swept I thought about his life before he knew me. What it must have been like to grow up in a small town, relatively poor, in a noisy apartment full of kids, people, and chaos. I wondered who swept the floor. I'm sure there were no warm homemade cookies waiting for him after school. I moved on to clean out the leftover containers from the fridge. What had his fridge been like? Full of food? I imagined cheap, unhealthy honeybuns from the corner store and two-for-one tacos at Jack in the Box. As I made the bed I wondered, *Did he have his own bed, or did he share one?*

"Hey, Victor," I called from across the house.

"Yeah?" he replied, distracted, as he was watching MTV.

"Did you have your own room growing up? Or your own bed?"

"Nah, I slept on the couch most of the time. Well, when we had a couch. We moved a lot. Why?" he queried.

"Just wondering," I answered, then continued cleaning and thinking while he went back to watching MTV. He was used to my random questions.

My thoughts began to slow as I scrubbed the kitchen counters. I felt the weightiness of this new issue. Mental illness was one thing, but drug use was quite another. I suspected something really rotten with this James person. Intuition I had in spades, and it rarely failed me, especially once I realized it had little to do with me and more to do with being in tune with God's Spirit. I was thinking perhaps now a new problem was staring me in the face.

I heated a cup of coffee and sat down at the kitchen table with my iPad and googled mental illness and drugs. Sipping my fragrant cup of dark roast, I began to read that, not surprisingly, 98 percent of people with mental disorders sought out illegal drugs. I sat back thoughtfully. *Well, what in the world do I do with this? I have even less experience with drugs than I do with mental illness.*

As I sat reading at the kitchen table, Victor came bouncing

out of his room. This was his "tell." He usually glides around the house, quiet on his feet like a cat, but when he is nervous he seems twice as big, and the jittery energy radiates from him. As he sat down at the table across from me, I reached up and hit the off button on the iPad.

"What you looking at?" he asked me, tapping his fingers on the table.

"Oh, just reading about how to deal with you, little brother." I looked at him dead-on, one eyebrow cocked.

"Nuh uh," he laughed nervously.

"Oh, yeah I am. Just remember, you don't get away with anything around here. You know I have eyes in the back of my head, right?"

"Hahaha," he laughed, but it did not reach his eyes. "Is it time to go yet? Is Dean ready?" His fingers were still dancing on the table.

"You sure you don't want to go with us to see Precious Granny?" I gave him one last chance, knowing he loved Granny.

"Naw naw, I'm good. I'll go see my friend."

I sat my now empty cup down on the table with a thump, frustration creating a tight band around the back of my neck. I was heartbroken that he was so deceived. "All right then, you want your friend? You will get your friend. I'll get my shoes."

I stalked into the bedroom where Dean was working at the desk and plopped down on the bed.

"You ready to go?" he asked, eyes on the computer.

"Yes, and our little friend Victor is ready too, to go to his friend's house and get all messed up so that later today when we get back home, I can deal with his messed-up self."

"Well," said Dean, "why don't you tell him he has to spend the night and go get him tomorrow? So you can get some rest."

"What?" I screeched. "Why would you offer to let him spend the night? I can't think of a worse idea! He could overdose, or worse yet, go back to the corner! Why would you ever even think to offer that to him?"

I could see immediately that my venting was not well received. Dean is a kind, gentle man, who listens to my never-ending flow of thoughts with patience almost all the time. He has calming words of wisdom and an unexpected point of view to almost any issue, particularly the kids and Victor. But every once in a while I go too far, press too much, and the stress gets to us. Then my words are not met with the usual calm smile. This was one of those times.

As I ranted on about Victor and the problem of the day, I could see his sweet face begin to cloud over, his lips clamping together in a tight line across his face. His eyes narrowed, and his body language shifted defensively. Even as I sat and watched his demeanor change, I somehow could not stop the torrent of words flowing from my mouth. Like a gushing geyser, I was standing outside of my body watching it happen and could not stop.

When I finally paused to breathe, it was his opportunity to share his feelings. "Well, since you know so much and know every nuance of how to handle Victor, although I have walked through every single step of this journey with you, why don't you just handle it yourself and stop telling me about it? I obviously don't know what I'm doing, and you know it all. Everything I say is wrong, and you fly off the handle when I make a suggestion." I have rarely seen anger flare in his eyes. *Uh oh.*

At that moment I suddenly realized how everything in my world had turned to revolve around Victor. Even when I consciously saw it happening, it was like the vortex surrounding a whirlwind that kept dragging me in. I stared at him for a moment, frustrated tears forming in my eyes. I wanted to be angry at him because I wanted to be angry at someone, and it was hard to be angry at Victor. And it was so much easier to lash out at someone standing in front of you than it was at a situation beyond your control.

As the tears hung at the edges of my eyelashes, I remembered how much I loved this man. How patient he had been, and how much of his time, freedom, money, and wife he has given up to help Victor. I remembered Ephesians 4:2: "Be completely humble and gentle." Yes, I thought about being mad back at him, but I also knew that these things—misplaced anger and frustration—can implode a marriage, having experienced them before. It was never far from my memory. I was determined not to let it happen to me again. Humility was my new friend. I took its hand and took a deep breath, remembering Proverbs 11:2, "When pride comes, then comes disgrace, but with humility comes wisdom."

I breathed a prayer and crossed the room to kneel by Dean's chair, placing my hand on his knee. "You're right, you know, I do fly off the handle. I just so desperately want to control the situation and protect him from any and all harm. It scares me to know that it's not possible. I have to trust the Lord to take care of it. Will you please forgive me?"

He remained still, stiff, and cranky. *Ah, it's one of those days.* I plucked his laptop from his hands and sat on his lap, wrapping my arms around his neck, forehead to his cheek. "Please forgive me, I know this is hard. I'm so sorry that it seems like you're on the back burner lately," I said quietly in his ear.

"It's fine," he said stonily.

As I sat there on his lap, I began to laugh. Oh, my goodness, I began to laugh until tears trickled down my face. He just stared at me unamused. "All right, Sprouse, well, I love you. I'm very sorry for what I said," I told him, as I lay my cheek briefly atop his head. I then went to collect Victor.

Why did I laugh? So many times, the Lord will send me a reminder of how my behavior affects other people by allowing me to experience it. I'm growing in my relationship with Christ as He gives gentle lessons. I understood His teaching right then. How many times have I done the same thing as Dean? Have someone apologize to me only to reject it, preferring instead to snuggle up tight with anger and hurt, hugging them close as if they will bring me some sort of comfort.

Now I knew that lie of the enemy, because that anger tore my first marriage apart, ripped it limb from limb. It was not going to happen here. I could get angry in return for his grumpiness and turn the whole thing into an awful day of silence, ignoring each other. Or, I could offer everything up to the Lord: my controlling tendencies, my fears, and my sweet husband and his grumpy face. I could then move on, go outside and enjoy the glorious sunshine, knowing that tomorrow is another day with problems of its own, and then, again, I would need the strength of the Lord to get me through it.

"So, you ready, Victor? Let's head out," I called.

We met Dean in the garage and I silently watched the guys load Victor's bike into the back of the Jeep. We all climbed in and Dean started the car. It was always curious to me that, just like my children, Victor was so attuned to our moods. When he sensed tension in the air, he would clam up and get busy with the knee jumping every time.

It was a quiet ride to James's house. As we pulled into the apartment complex, Victor was about ready to jump out of the car before we even came to a complete stop. "You know I need to meet your friend before I let you stay here, right? Like he needs to come down here and meet me," I said sternly.

"I'll ask him," Victor answered dubiously. "I don't know if he'll come down." Away he went, bounding up to the third floor, two steps at a time.

I sat there and watched. Dean hit the button for the hatchback and exited the Jeep, the door slamming shut as I turned his way. Still angry. *How is it that I'm sitting here in this parking lot, on this day, dealing with all of this?* I asked the Lord. I took a deep breath, asked the Father to help me remember what humility and grace looked like, and got out of the car. Dean was sitting under the hatchback, sunglasses on, legs swinging.

"Still mad?" I asked, hopping up beside him.

He exhaled, looking at the pavement. "Not really. Just gets old, you know?"

"Yes, I know," I agreed. "But we can't quit."

He turned and looked at me.

"Who else is going to take care of him?" I asked quietly. "I just know we can't let all of this drama interfere with our marriage. That's priority."

"Yes," he said. "It is."

I leaned my head on his shoulder and enjoyed the sun on my face. For a moment all was well. About that time, I heard heavy clomping on the stairs. "All right, let's get this over with," I said.

I hopped up and walked around the side of the car expecting a short, thug-looking type with a leather jacket and multiple gold chains, and maybe even a bandana around his head with a gang symbol. Too many after-school movies perhaps? I came face-to-face with James. He was older, sixtyish maybe, tall, skinny, with a gold chain but no medallions in sight. He was wearing a white undershirt and a faded pair of short blue workout pants. He had glasses on and a small, brown, bug-eyed Chihuahua tucked under one arm.

He bent over and set the little dog on the ground. "That's Coco. I'm James," he said in a singsong voice, slightly effeminate. He stuck his hand out with a polite, friendly smile.

I stepped forward, cautiously, not as warm and friendly as he. "Hi, I'm Ginger. What's your last name?" I asked, not so friendly.

"Green. It's James Green," he provided, still smiling.

But I wasn't buying it; this was too bizarre. What did this older gentleman want with Victor? "How do you know Victor?" I asked.

"I've been seeing him on the corner for years now. My girlfriend and I used to wash his clothes sometimes," he responded promptly.

"How nice," I replied, thinking back to what Victor had told me, that this friend would come pick him up sometimes and take him to a club downtown and buy him drinks. The Victor I knew from the corner was a filthy, stinking mess; not to mention, barely coherent enough to hold a conversation many days. And this guy was washing his clothes? Taking him clubbing? I was not buying this friendly act. Still, in my best tough voice, looking him square in the eye, I said, "Well, Mr. Green, it is certainly nice to meet you. I meet all of Victor's friends, you know. I always make sure that everyone who comes around him is on the up and up, you know? Can't have anyone with ill intent hanging out."

"He's alright, alright. We cool here. No problems," Victor jumped in. He was a bundle of nerves that day.

As Mr. Green and I continued to size each other up, there was a strange zing in the air between us. I looked over his shoulder and saw Dean standing there in the sunlight, one hand on the hatchback. He knew my not-having-it tone and gave me a slight nod.

"Well, Mr. Green, I would surely like to see where you live and meet your girlfriend."

"We don't have to do all that," said Victor nervously. "I'm good, you can go now."

"No, I don't think so. I'm sure Mr. Green won't mind at all, will you?" I challenged.

"Oh, no Miss Ginger," he responded politely. "That's just fine by me. You can meet Miranda, my girlfriend."

"I would be delighted."

I turned on my heel and headed up the stairs, leaving James and Victor to follow. As I rounded the corner I looked down at Dean and got a thumbs-up and a smile. *Geez, what am I doing?* I wondered. This was the kind of day when I should have been in my bathing suit, in the middle of the lake in a boat, with a cold glass of iced tea in one hand and my toes in the water. Too late now. I stopped in front of a propped-open screen door and stepped to the side to allow James to enter before me. I saw Victor bringing up the rear, with the little brown dog firmly attached by the teeth to his pant leg, growling. He was dragging his leg behind him as he walked.

"Um, the dog is biting you, Victor," I said.

"Aw naw, she's not biting, she's playing. She loves me."

I cocked an eyebrow. "Really?"

The dog then let go of his pants and ran at me, teeth bared. I stomped my foot in her face. "I think not, short legs. I'll send you over the railing if you bite me." She stopped, did an about-face, and ran into the apartment, settling between James's legs.

"She's just spicy that way," James simpered, giggling weirdly.

I walked by him uninvited into the apartment. It reeked of

cigarette smoke. There was a middle-aged African American woman sitting on the couch with another Chihuahua on her lap. This one was brown and old and tired looking. One sad tooth hung limply out of the side of its mouth. The woman was patting him absently.

I walked to her and held out my hand. "Hi, I hear you are Miranda. Nice to meet you."

"Mmm hmm," she mumbled, placing her palm limply in mine.

She just bobbed her head, not rising from the couch. Her mass of curls dipped around her face as she tipped her chin toward me. Her eyes were red and bloodshot, and she had a faded beauty about her. She smiled slightly, and I could see her teeth were dark and stained. I squeezed her hand briefly, and she let it fall heavily back into her lap. Yes, she was on something. Who knows what. And I was really thinking of leaving Victor here with these people? I stepped back and almost landed on James's foot.

"Don't you worry about Miss Miranda here. We was just up a little late last night and she's real tired," he singsonged at me, flitting over to the kitchen table across the room.

I walked toward him as Victor nervously hopped from one foot to the other in front of the door. My senses jangled, knowing that this was a bad place. I walked to a sliding glass door, covered top to bottom in smudges but looking out over Clear Lake with a stunning view of the water. Standing with my back to the room, I remarked, "How fortunate you get to look at this amazing view every day."

"Ah, yes, Miss Ginger, been living here going on twelve years now."

"Really?" I remarked. "Good to know." I turned slowly,

trying to take a picture in my mind and listen to every detail I could, lingering as long as possible before Victor imploded with nervousness.

"You see, we all good people here, you don't have nothing to worry about." James smiled at me, an edge to his high-pitched voice.

"No, guess I don't after all." I smiled thinly, looking him in the eye. "Doesn't mean I won't keep checking. Better now, though, since I know where you live, right?" There was a slight edge of challenge in my voice.

James crossed the room and stood with his hand on the doorknob, ready to usher me out. Victor stood on the other side of the door, and I could see he was very ready for me to leave. Stopping in front of him, I asked one last time, "You sure you don't want to go with us to Precious's house? We are having barbecue, and you know how much she loves you."

He patted me awkwardly on the shoulder, embarrassed, pushing and patting me out the door at the same time. "I'm good, I'm good. I'll be home later, you know."

I gave in. "Oh, I know you will. And if not, I know where you are."

As I walked out, I heard laughing and the sound of palms slapping as the screen door swung shut soundly behind me. I shook my head to clear the scene from my mind, but knew it was a fruitless exercise. The tension that lived at all times in the back of my neck stretched itself and wrapped a few more tendrils around the muscles there.

I headed down the stairs to where Dean was waiting by the car. He was leaning back, face to the cloudless blue sky with his ankles crossed. "Well? Your baby going to be okay?" he asked.

"Who knows," I said wearily. "Can we just get in the car and drive, and go somewhere where no one knows us or Victor? So if he goes back to the corner and it all goes badly wrong, no one will blame me or expect me to fix it?"

He laughed. "Well, you can, but you'll have to take yourself with you. You know, and I know, too, that you could never live with that."

"Yeah, I know. My sense of responsibility can be so annoying. Let's go see your mom and eat some barbecue. There's nothing more we can do here today except pray."

I did pray, then enjoyed time with family and ate barbeque. What else was there to do? Victor returned home that night relatively unscathed, if not a bit loopy. All the tension and drama fizzled, leaving us all a bit drained, but relieved.

CHAPTER 16

Looking in the Mirror

I sometime use a pressure cooker when I teach cooking classes. It always amuses me that most of my students have a deadly fear of them. The rattling knob on top and the steam screaming from beneath as the pressure builds sends them running in fear every time. Lots of days my life feels like that—like I'm in a pressure cooker. After ten months of living with Victor, making time for my family, and running my business, the pressure was getting to me. It was building, the gauge was rattling, and things were threatening to blow.

But I would never have guessed that after walking through all the difficult steps with Victor—getting his state ID card, Social Security card, and birth certificate; scheduling his doctors' and family visits; and enduring the tension in my home with the added stress of a new roommate—the thing that would absolutely be my undoing would come from outside of our home. I felt as if the

Lord was allowing me to feel some of the betrayal and hurt that Ben had experienced.

Although I had been deliberately ignoring it for many months, hoping it would go away on its own, I knew that the TV and radio interviews were eliciting quite a bit of "talk" on social media. One bit of advice: if you ever have the opportunity to experience the proverbial "fifteen minutes of fame," do not, under any circumstances, google your own name. What a horrendous mistake I made.

One afternoon Aaron and I were sitting in the kitchen casually talking and laughing about all the changes that we had experienced in the last few months. We were reading some articles online, marveling at the amount of inaccuracies in some news stories. It was laughable really, seeing what was written about us and comparing them to the everyday normal lives we led. Then we stumbled upon a particular social media posting and began to read the comments.

The overwhelming majority were positive. People were happy that Victor was doing well, that he was feeling good and had somewhere to stay. However, as Aaron wandered off to call a friend, I continued to scroll down the page. I was horrified to see the negative comments left there on the screen for all the world to see: Dean and I were out to get famous off Victor's name; I had created the "This Is Victor" page to let everyone know what a "good" person I was; and the worst was the insinuation that we were out to make money from the GoFundMe account. I sat and felt my face grow hot and my stomach twist into knots, then tears began to course down my cheeks. This was wrong. This is not what I wanted! Why could I not have done something nice and not told anyone about it?

My intention for the media and TV interviews had been to

sing the praises of the Father and all He had accomplished. From the outside, I suppose it was easy to think that the interviews were intended to show everyone the good things we had done. Many of us crave recognition for the good deeds we do. I, though, wanted to learn what the humility Jesus showed me looked like. I began daily to ask the Lord to prune away any sense of pride in my involvement with Victor. I felt confirmation that this was the Lord's project, and He had graciously allowed me to have a part in it. I knew the truth: without the hand of God on Victor's life, this would not have happened, regardless of how many well-intentioned people were involved.

Online commentaries on a Facebook post or a blog are one thing—you can choose not to seek them out or look at them—but accusations from someone you trust is quite another. What I learned is that pride can lie coiled like a snake, quietly dormant until poked, striking when you least expect it.

On the first Thanksgiving Day after Victor came to live with us, Jillian, one of the well-meaning acquaintances we had made when we introduced Victor to our community, stood in my driveway next to her shiny blue Toyota Camry. She and I met soon after the creation of Victor's Facebook page, and we had spoken often of Victor's trials and what could be done; she had spent some time with Victor too. But as the months progressed, and my need for her help waned, she became increasingly remote. She had her own ideas about what should be done for Victor and was quite vocal about them. Dean and I found many of her ideas helpful, but at the end of the day, we made our decisions based on our wisdom and the guidance from the Lord. Looking back now, I suppose I did a poor job of communicating our thought process with her, which left her feeling hurt and me angry and resentful that she did not understand my situation. Satan does so enjoy hurt feelings and uses them to his ugly advantage, many times with us as willing participants.

Dean and I were headed out to the cooking school that morning to spend time with our extended "family." In the last two years, it had become a tradition for us to invite our homeless friends in the community for Thanksgiving dinner at the cooking school. It was a fun-filled kickoff to our holiday season. Many families have drama-filled holidays, but we, with our sweet friends from the street, would spend a relaxing day sharing a hot meal, swapping stories, and just being grateful to know one another. And many of these people knew Victor from the street, so I wanted to make sure he was there to help serve, not only to remind him of how far he had come but also to give some hope and encouragement to our friends. Unfortunately, that never came to pass this Thanksgiving Day.

Jillian looked lovely, standing in our driveway that Thanksgiving morning to pick up Victor for lunch. Her dark hair gleamed in the afternoon sun under the sunglasses perched atop her head. She was dressed to the nines in a yellow polka-dot sundress, her perfectly pink manicured toes peeking out of the front of her pretty high-heeled sandals. But the picture standing there in front of us was in sharp contrast to what was being said from her pink painted lips. Those lips were twisted in an ugly snarl, and her anger caused her lovely face to contort and her forehead to crease with furious lines. Her usual sweetly lilting tone with the light Southern accent was harsh, demanding, and loud. She stabbed the air angrily with her pink fingertip as she proceeded to accuse us of being liars, stealing money from Victor, using him to promote our business, keeping him from seeing his friends, and seeking to get famous by using him in the media.

I stared at her, surprised at her anger, and gave Dean a sideways glance. He, too, had a deer-in-the-headlights expression. Jillian declared that her next step was to contact the media and tell them "what we were doing." Having no desire to stand in the line of fire any longer, I turned and walked away. As I opened the door Victor guiltily jumped back from the window.

"Is she mad?" he asked worriedly. He very much enjoyed his lunch outings with Jillian.

"Well, she's a little wound up," I downplayed, not wanting to upset him. "She'll be fine. Make sure you guys get ice cream. That makes everything better, right?" I smiled as I gave him a squeeze and held the door open.

I saw her straighten and move quickly toward Victor with a huge smile, leaving Dean forgotten beside her car. He beat a hasty retreat to the garage while she ushered Victor to the passenger side of the car. I stood there and watched them drive away. Then I leaned back against the door and asked the Lord out loud, "Did I do something wrong here?" I felt exhaustion wash over me.

For weeks the cruel comments on social media kept me up at night, tormenting me. And now here was someone I knew feeling the same way. I feared what was coming next. I knew from my study of Scripture how the Lord was asking me to handle this matter. Ephesians 4:32 did not mince words: "be kind to each other, tenderhearted, forgiving one another, just as God through Christ has forgiven you" (NLT). I also tried to remind myself of Proverbs 27:6: "Wounds from a sincere friend are better than many kisses from an enemy" (NLT).

I have a friend who speaks often of "teachable moments." Well, if there was ever a time for those moments, this was it. But to be honest, as I stood there a black anger boiled up inside me. I looked at my hand on the doorknob, then heaved the door as hard as I could; the deafening slam rattled the windows and sent the dogs running for cover. I was having a moment all right. The enemy was right there, whispering again. Everything in me was screaming to retaliate. *My family has given up so much! Our home, our time, our privacy, our finances. And this is the thanks I get? Accused of stealing? Wanting fame? Surely if I wanted to get rich and famous I could come up with something easier than adopting a homeless person who had so much need!*

I was so very angry. I marched into the bathroom and slammed that door as well. It felt good. I locked it tight behind me, then turned on the shower and let the hot water run so it would drown out the ugly torrent of words flooding from my mouth; all the things I had wanted to say to her. I ranted on, punching my fist in the air and waving my arms, tension taking over my body as I expressed all the frustration that was inside of me. As I raged, I turned and saw my reflection in the mirror.

Much like Jillian, my hair gleamed under the light of the mirrored vanity, with my sunglasses perched on top of my head. My lips, though not lined in pink, were twisted in anger, and the lines across my face were deepened. I looked to my extended hand and saw my manicured fingers. I dropped my hand quickly to my side as though I had touched something hot. And as quickly as my hand had fallen, I hit my knees on the damp bath mat, right there in the steamy bathroom.

The Spirit of God within me was not going to let this pass. This was it. This was the moment I had to press on, love as I had been called or swill about in this abyss of anger and resentment, the root of which was pride, pride, pride. Oh, it does go before the fall. Why in the world could I not learn this lesson once and for all? Even there on my knees, tears streaming down my face, the flesh inside me screamed that it was not fair, that they were all lies and they hurt. I did not want to forgive or love her. But I knew that if I wanted to accept what God was teaching me, I must. Then, just as quickly, James 1:22–24 rose up from the ugliness inside, reminding me,

> But don't just listen to God's word. You must do what it says. Otherwise, you are only fooling yourselves. For if you listen to the word and don't obey, it is like glancing at your face in a mirror. You see yourself, walk away, and forget what you look like. (NLT)

I immediately sat up. I had seen my image in the mirror, and it was ugly. I lifted myself up to my knees and scooted closer to the vanity, then I rose, slowly, peeking over the edge of the countertop. I saw my red-rimmed eyes, mascara running down my cheeks, carpet marks on my forehead. This was not a good look. I wanted the look of someone full of the Holy Spirit described in Galatians 5:22–23. The one that produced love, joy, peace, patience, kindness, goodness, faithfulness, gentleness, and self-control. I knew those fruits would never produce something like the mess I saw staring back at me that day.

I sat back down on my knees for a few minutes, my chin propped on the vanity counter. Right there in that bathroom, I repented. Again. It would not be the last time, as the enemy of my soul follows me about, screaming that my past would never let me go. But thankfully I have a kind and loving Father who disciplines me, and I wanted to hear His voice. The consequences of my sin too painful to bear alone, I prayed for guidance. I was reminded of Hebrews 12:10–14:

> For our earthly fathers disciplined us for a few years, doing the best they knew how. But God's discipline is always good for us, so that we might share in his holiness. No discipline is enjoyable while it is happening—it's painful! But afterward there will be a peaceful harvest of right living for those who are trained in this way.
>
> So take a new grip with your tired hands and strengthen your weak knees. Mark out a straight path for your feet so that those who are weak and lame will not fall but become strong.
>
> Work at living in peace with everyone, and work at living a holy life, for those who are not holy will not see the Lord. (NLT)

The sweet song the Bible sings to me is one of grace. And I have learned to give grace, not perfectly by any means, but better with time. I have learned to quietly be with the Word and read verses, chapters, whole books at a time, like a novel, even the Old Testament, again and again and again. Real change began in me with a love for the Word of God, and only then did I begin to understand that God forgave, He desired to restore relationships, and He yearned for people to repent and listen.

So many times I had thought in my heart that God did not want any of us to have any fun, that He wanted us to just blindly obey and have stilted, boring lives. But I learned that all these things—anger, bitterness, and resentment—I carried around and could not let go were heavy; they were like lead weights for the soul. There was something to be said for looking outside of oneself and being free of that weight. That's what I had asked of the Lord regarding Victor: to teach me to love others the way He does. I just had no idea that it was much easier to love someone so different, with dirty fingernails and smelly clothes and all, than it was to love someone so like me.

I still practice grace. It's a daily discipline, and it's hard. Jillian never spoke to me again. So there still lies tattered on the ground an ugly, unreconciled former friendship. But Victor loves her, and they continue to have their lunch dates. It shames me to see how easily he loves and forgives. I know God gives that unrelenting grace to all, and only through Him will there be healing, one day.

It's a tapestry God is weaving in our lives. A tapestry of grace. The golden threads woven in among the dirty ones I created. It grows as I do, as Victor has. We sit quietly each night, Victor and I, with Bibles on our knees, taking turns reading out loud the truths of God's Word. Victor calls it "Bible time." We pray, too, for one another, our family, our enemies, our friends, and most of all, for God's will to be done. Then we get up and hug, wishing each other good night, and then the next day it is on to real life.

I want with all my heart and soul to continue on this journey with my Lord. I don't like the times when He feels far away, when I feel I have given enough and want to just sit back and rest. Jesus gave tirelessly while His feet touched the dusty roads, as He traveled on this earth He created. He was weary. And what did He do in His weariness? He retreated to the wilderness to be with His Father. That is where He found His refreshment, like drinking from a beautiful pool of fresh, clear water. He ate of the very Word of God, His Father. He is my Father too, and I also have the privilege of drinking from the pool and eating of the Word, which nourishes and keeps me going when I think I'm done. I'm so grateful.

The instructions of the Lord are perfect,
reviving the soul.
The decrees of the Lord are trustworthy,
making wise the simple.
The commandments of the Lord are right,
bringing joy to the heart.
The commands of the Lord are clear,
giving insight for living.
Reverence for the Lord is pure,
lasting forever.
The laws of the Lord are true;
each one is fair.
They are more desirable than gold,
even the finest gold.
They are sweeter than honey,
even honey dripping from the comb.
They are a warning to your servant,
a great reward for those who obey them.

(Ps. 19:7–11 NLT)

And the Lord is gracious. He allows us to see the fruit. I see how our reaching out has compelled others to seek to lend a hand to the less fortunate. I see how Victor's kindness and his smile that lights up a room have inspired people to give those on the street a second look. I love to see the fruit of kindness and compassion growing in our city and across the world, as stories pour in from people who have stepped out and stepped up.

Epilogue

It is New Year's Eve 2017, and I'm sitting in a hotel room on the twenty-second floor in Manhattan. The lights of New York City spread out before me like millions of bright, twinkling stars, but the backlight of my computer is the only light in the room. Dean, Aaron, and Victor are out exploring the city, while I am alone in the room. The silence is welcome. In an hour we will be among the guests of honor at the Lincoln Center, at a party thrown by yet another media outlet. It is a surreal experience outside of our routine lives. I'm thinking about the coming New Year. *What does the Lord have in store for us?*

Victor is stable and happy. He is now working at Chick-fil-A near our house. Feeling a need to move forward, he walked into the restaurant on his own and filled out an application. There, in the dining room, his sweet personality shines as he greets the guests and makes sure their drinks are filled. Every day he returns from work beaming with pride. He still talks to his mother, and the conversations are more positive; perhaps she is getting used to the idea that Victor is part of our family too.

I'm still working at the cooking school, Dean is still remodeling homes, and Nicki and Aaron are at college. My relationship with my kids is getting better; the painful wounds of the past are healing and will continue to do so.

Life is short, and there is little time to pat myself on the back. James 4:14 resonates in my mind: "Why, you do not even know what will happen tomorrow. What is your life? You are a mist that appears for a little while and then vanishes." If that is true, there is much to accomplish. I have time later, maybe at the end of my life, to say with the apostle Paul, "I have fought the good fight, I have finished the race, I have kept the faith" (2 Tim. 4:7). Until then, "I press on toward the goal to win the prize for which God has called me heavenward in Christ Jesus" (Phil. 3:14).

I click on the reading lamp, and as the twinkling lights outside the window disappear, I see my reflection on the glass. A little older, a lot wiser, and at last a committed grown-up willing to look at her past mistakes right in the eye and see what was there: unrepentant sin. It consumed the life I had and burned it to smoldering embers. But the promise of the Old Testament gives hope:

> To all who mourn in Israel,
> he will give a crown of beauty for ashes,
> a joyous blessing instead of mourning,
> festive praise instead of despair.
> In their righteousness, they will be like great oaks
> that the LORD has planted for his own glory.
>
> (ISA. 61:3 NLT)

This verse reminds me, as it does every day, that I am a person who was taken by the hand of God and shown grace, despite the fact that I once threw away everything I had to chase a lie. I am forgiven. Yes, I will sin again, but the Holy Spirit gently chides, and repentance will come with a grateful heart. So now I resolve to spend the rest of my days telling others of the One who died for me and gave me a second chance at life, just as He did for Victor.

~

I realize that the next day, New Year's Day, will be one year to the day that Dean and I put Victor in a hotel room. A lot of life has happened since then, and through it all the Lord has kept us safe and sane. Despite seemingly insurmountable obstacles, He has wrought many miracles. As I read my Bible verse of the day, I shake my head slowly, and then I begin to chuckle. As it sinks in, I throw my head back and laugh until I have tears streaming down my face. Just then, Dean walks in and turns on the light.

"What's so funny?" he asks, bemused.

I gesture to the Bible. "Here, read this, it's part of my reading for today."

As I walk to the mirror to fix my mascara and apply my lipstick, he reads aloud:

> And here is my judgment about what is best for you in this matter. Last year you were the first not only to give but also to have the desire to do so. Now finish the work, so that your eager willingness to do it may be matched by your completion of it, according to your means. (2 Cor. 8:10–11)

"Wow. God really talks to you, doesn't He?" Dean asks quietly.

Yes. Yes, He does, in that still, small voice. And I'm listening. I smile and extend my hand. "What do you say we go collect the boys and usher in the New Year?"

He takes my hand in his and we shut the door behind us as we make our way down the hall to see what the Lord has in store for us.

It's 2018, and as my children are pursuing their own dreams, beginning their own lives, Dean and I are moving forward in ours, with Victor held close to us. I don't speak of my dreams often, for I am abundantly blessed already. And yet, ever since the day I closed the door on my old life and walked away, I have secretly dreamed in my heart of having a little farm again, with my beloved animals and happy family around me.

Then, out of the clear blue sky came a beautiful, sweet gift from my heavenly Father: a new home. It is a sweet little farm on several acres, with a small farmhouse and a falling-down barn. The best part is the tiny little guesthouse, ten steps from our back door, which will be Victor's house. His very own place. The night we sat him down to share our plans with him is the sweetest of pictures, one I will always treasure in my heart.

He was in his bedroom, the room that is a mere ten steps from ours, which he has called his since the day he graduated from a guest on our living room floor to a family member. As usual, he was perched on the edge of the bed, ready to jump up at a moment's notice in the event someone needed him. It was his day off from work, and he had donned his typical day-at-home attire of gray long-john bottoms and white tank top with white crew socks. The ever-present MTV played quietly in the background, emanating a warm glow against the dark blue walls, his favorite color. It gives the room a cozy feel. He is a creature of habit, our Victor. His favorite things surrounding him give him great comfort and peace. We had deliberately not told him that we were moving, because "maybes" causes worry and unease for my little brother, as we have learned over the last year.

But now that this new little farmhouse was ours, papers signed, keys in hand, and packing boxes stowed in the back of my Jeep, it was time to let him know our plans. We hoped he would be happy about the move. I had prayed so many times asking God to please send someone to take care of him as I drove by his corner, and here he sat, an answered prayer. I plopped down beside him on the bed and smiled.

"Hey homie, what you up to?" I asked, patting my sweet friend on the back. Dean settled himself comfortably on Victor's desk chair across from us.

He turned and looked at me suspiciously. "What's wrong?"

"Nothing's wrong." I laughed, trying to put him at ease. I suppose our serious conversations have always been preceded by me sitting there beside him and Dean opposite in the chair. Inadvertently, the serious Mom look came out, and it immediately set him on edge.

"Did something bad happen?" His brow creased in concern. I would have loved to have been able to ease into the big news, but knew it was better to rip off the Band-Aid quickly.

"Hold out your hand," I said with a smile.

"Why? What you going to do? Don't put anything slimy in my hand!" He sat with hands tightly pressed between his knees.

I laughed at his antics. "No, nothing slimy. A surprise." I tugged his arm gently and placed a brand-new shiny key in his palm.

He stared at it. "What's this?"

"That, little brother, is the key to your brand-new little house. We are moving, and you're invited to come with us if you want to!"

Dean jumped in, "Look here, we took some pictures to show you. It's your own little house. Your front door is ten steps from ours. Only a little farther than your room is right now."

Victor sat quietly for a moment looking at the pictures, then staring at the key in his hand. He raised his dark brown eyes to meet mine, a slight crease between his brows. "You really want me to come with you?" he asked softly, looking right into my heart.

The tears quickly clouded my vision. Around the lump in my throat I said simply, "Yes. You are our family. We will not leave you."

He looked at Dean, who cleared his throat and nodded. We all sat quietly for a moment as Victor's fingers slowly closed around the key. He nodded firmly, his face lighting up with a relieved smile. "Yes, I'll come. I'll come home with you."

The next hour was a torrent of questions. "Dean," Victor queried, "what was it like when you moved out of your mother's house, you know, on your own? Like I will be in my new house. Was it scary?"

It dawned on me then what a huge deal this was to Victor. Even though he was a mere ten steps from my door, he was going to be on his own. That frightened him a little, but his eyes were bright and shining as he talked about choosing paint colors and getting a new dresser.

"Oh, my goodness!" he suddenly exclaimed. "I need to buy an ironing board!"

I laughed. "Really? I've never seen you iron. But by all means, if you need an ironing board we will make that happen."

"And a puppy! I can get a puppy too."

"Uh, ah," I stammered a little, "I don't know about that. Maybe we can get settled in first?" I placated.

He patted me knowingly on the shoulder. "That's okay, I know you need to see if I'm responsible first. We can start out with a fish tank."

"Exactly, little brother. A fish tank it is." I smiled, relieved. This was going to be just fine.

Three of us sat together that evening as a family, pouring over the photographs of our new home, making plans, and talking about the future. It was a glorious night. I was reminded,

> Then Christ will make his home in your hearts as you trust in him. Your roots will grow down into God's love and keep you strong. And may you have the power to understand, as all God's people should, how wide, how long, how high, and how deep his love is. May you experience the love of Christ, though it is too great to understand fully. Then you will be made complete with all the fullness of life and power that comes from God.
>
> Now all glory to God, who is able, through his mighty power at work within us, to accomplish infinitely more than we might ask or think. (Eph. 3:17–20 NLT)

Acknowledgments

To Rachel Sussman, without you there would be no book. Thank you for following up, even after I kept deleting your emails! Thank you for the idea and the encouragement, and for shepherding an idea into a proposal and acquisition so Victor's grace-filled story could be shared with the world. Your patience and professionalism made this process (almost) painless. You were instrumental in God's plan from day one.

To my editor, Jenny Baumgartner, I know the words contained here were edited by Spirit-filled fingers. Thank you so much for your kind guidance, friendship, and a wonderful experience.

To the people of Clear Lake, Texas, many of whom had been taking care of Victor for years. The outpouring of love and compassion for Victor that continues to this very day has been stunning. The generosity of each and every one of you has made it possible for us to have the strength to carry on in the discouraging days. It delights me to see the joy Victor brings to you all. From the deepest recesses of my heart, thank you.

To Chief Shipp, Todd Weidman, and the firefighters at Webster Fire Department, you guys are rock stars. Long before I ever stopped and noticed Victor, you watched over him and then walked by my side for months through all the "stuff." Not only did you guys show up every night, but you really cared. I'm honored and proud to call you friends.

To the staff of Chick-fil-A on Hwy 96, thank you for taking such good care of Victor, and teaching him what hard work is all about with such sweet kindness.

To Slow Twiche Niche, the Victor 5000 is the classiest bike in the neighborhood. He treasures it.

To Julie Y, maybe someday he will wear his glasses.

To Lynn, I'm still having "teachable moments" every day. Thank you for your support, my Cajun friend.

To Jennifer, with three little ones you still make time for Victor. You are an inspiration to me and a true example of a mother raising her children with grace and truth. I'm so glad Victor has Landon as his best friend.

To my "merciful" friend, who has helped so much and yet always declines to be recognized. What an example of humility you are to me. I would not have made it through without your prayers.

To Julie and April, Victor loves you. Thank you for your help.

To Jacob, you have loved Victor well, and continue to do so. You make me so proud.

To my homie, you are my family. We will never leave you. I love your face.

About the Author

Ginger Sprouse is a wife, mother, chef, and small business owner of Art of the Meal. You can read more about her on the Art of the Meal website: artofthemeal.net/our-story. She lives in the Texas Hill Country with her husband, Dean, and little brother, Victor.

Victor's home on the corner of El Camino Real and Nasa Road 1 in Clear Lake, Texas, where I met him. Aaron took the photo from our car on November 2016.

By March 2017, Victor was living with Dean and me, and we were adjusting to one another. What a wonderful reminder.

Victor and Dean jet skiing at the family Easter gathering in 2017. Dean said he laughed the entire time. How wonderful it is to see him smile.

Victor and Dean visiting me at work, June 2017.

Victor enjoying a beautiful day in downtown Houston, June 2018.

Victor and I having a little fun outing at the zoo, June 2018.

Victor sitting on the front steps of his very own home, September 2018.

(*Left to right:* Aaron, me, Victor, Dean) An exciting family trip to New York City, New Year's Eve 2018.